# TAKING MORE THAN A COMMISSION

## A Critique of the Commission Agent System in Punjab Agriculture

# TAKING MORE THAN A COMMISSION

## A Critique of the Commission Agent System in Punjab Agriculture

Sukhpal Singh
Tejinder K. Dhaliwal

# TAKING MORE THAN A COMMISSION

A Critique of the Commission Agent System in Punjab Agriculture

Sukhpal Singh
Tejinder K. Dhaliwal



First Published, 2011

ISBN 978-93-5002-106-4



*Published by*
**AAKAR BOOKS**
28 E Pocket IV, Mayur Vihar Phase I, Delhi-110 091
Phone : 011-2279 5505 Telefax : 011-2279 5641
aakarbooks@gmail.com; www.aakarbooks.com

*Printed at*
Mudrak, Delhi-110 091

# CONTENTS

# FOREWORD

"*Taking More than a Commission: A Critique of the Commission Agent System in Punjab Agriculture*' by Dr Sukhpal Singh and Dr Tejinder K. Dhaliwal is an important academic intervention on a key area in the agrarian economy and society of Punjab. It throws light on the changing role of the commission agent, popularly known as *arhtiya*. Historically, the commission agent has been a key player in two inter-linked markets: the product market and the credit market. It seems that the growth in the economic power of the commission agent is now leading to their entry into the land market with money-rich commission agents buying the land of debt-ridden farmers. This study provides rich empirical evidence to the commonly held perception that, as commission agents are accumulating wealth, a large number of farmers are being driven into indebtedness leading, in many cases, to dispossession of land. An important finding of this study is that with assured marketing of important crops at predetermined prices and the emergence of financial institutions, the old role of the commission agent as a facilitator for marketing of agricultural produce and the provider of credit has become less crucial if not totally redundant.

An important policy implication of this study is that farmers need to be paid directly for marketing of their produce and not through the commission agents. This will facilitate the unshackling of the economic and social stranglehold of the commission agents-cum-moneylenders over the farmers. This empowering of the farmer can be further facilitated by the provision of institutional credit at reasonable rates of interest. This study has highlighted that the commission agents not only charge exorbitant rates of interest on the credit provided to the farmers, but many of them also make use of unethical practices such as under-weighing of agricultural produce through manipulation in the weighing process.

I strongly endorse the recommendation of this study that alternative marketing systems such as the Direct State Procurement and Cooperative Marketing System need to be developed to save Punjab agriculture from further ruin and to stop the ongoing process of forced depeasantisation and pauperisation in Punjab's countryside.

This study deserves wide dissemination in the wider public, critical attention by the academic community, and acceptance of its recommendations by the policy planners.

**Dr Pritam Singh**
Director
Postgraduate Programme in International Management
and International Relations
Oxford Brookes University
Oxford, UK

# PREFACE

A commission agent, commonly referred to as *arhtiya*, performs the function of a mediator between farmers and buyers for the marketing of agricultural produce. In view of the deepening agrarian crisis in Punjab and the role of arhtiyas, particularly in the light of the existing mode of payment of agricultural produce to the farmers, the present study has been conducted to understand the grip of the arhtiyas on the Punjab peasantry. The study also questions the prevalent informal credit market and recommends measures to loosen the stranglehold of the commission agent system as a step in favour of the hard working peasantry of Punjab.

The complexity of the relationship between the commission agents and farmers has undergone changes, especially during the declining phase of the green revolution. Now arhtiyas are fighting to retain what has been traditionally referred to as the *Nauh Maas Da Rista*—nail and flesh relationship—with the farmers. The farmers of the state are fighting back to break these age old ties, saying these have kept them as bonded, indebted, and distressed. The growing dependency of the farmer on the arhtiya for a steady flow of cash inputs goes beyond the needs of agricultural inputs only as the survival of peasant families is under threat and farm households depend on arhtiyas to fulfil various other familial and social needs. In this context, the malpractices and manipulations of the arhtiyas have reached an extent that would be unimaginable to an outsider but form the daily reality of thousands of peasant families in the state. Any attempt to loosen the grip of the arhtiyas on the peasantry necessitates the search for alternatives because the commercialization of agriculture and the increasing need of cash inputs are reaching heights.

On the recommendation of the Punjab Sate Farmers Commission, the Punjab Relief of Agricultural Indebtedness Bill, 2006 was drafted at the very end of the previous Congress government. However, the Bill has not seen the light of day despite approval from the cabinet. Even the present government has submitted in the Punjab and Haryana High Court that the enactment of the draft legislation is 'under consideration'. This matter had come up in the public interest litigation on farmers' suicides in Punjab. Similarly, the issue of direct payment to farmers without the involvement of the arhtiyas is also in the High Court. All the farmers' associations want direct payment and the enactment of the Farm Bill, through which the farmers can get relief from arhtiyas. Some academicians have highlighted that the arhtiya system has lost its significance and relevance in this changing world economic order. The present study is an effort to address this complicated issue from multiple directions so that argument and opinion could be built in a rightful manner.

The wide-spectrum view from the farmers' side is loud and clear. Farmers want the arhtiyas out. Ajmer Singh Lakhowal, Chairman, Punjab Mandi Board and President, Bhartiya Kisan Union (BKU), strongly holds the view that there should be 'online' direct payment to the farmers for their produce. According to him and many others, the farmer is the owner of the produce and the government is the buyer, so where is the place for the arhtiyas? Except BKU (Rajewal), almost all the factions of farmer organizations, academicians, and procurement agencies are in favour of direct payment to the farmers. Nevertheless, payment is still being made indirectly through the arhtiyas. Why? Our book explores the various dimensions of the arhtiya system and attempts to suggest an alternative marketing system through which the exploitation of the peasantry could be checked.

The whole discussion is divided into six chapters. The issues of origin and growth of the arhtiya system have been elaborated in the introductory Chapter 1, in which various acts and laws related to land and debt of peasantry are discussed. Although the Punjab peasantry has been reeling under debt since ages, the green revolution has increased their debt intensity and the severity of crisis. This chapter also includes sampling design, approaches, concepts, and definitions used in the study. The status of the commission agent system in Punjab agriculture has been studied in Chapter 2. The changing scenario of the commission agent system has been presented in Chapter 3, which also highlights the changes taking place on account of caste, allied occupations, and various professional and unprofessional practices. Chapter 4 incorporates the perceptions and viewpoints of commission agents and farmers regarding the relevance of the arhtiya system in the context of the increasing commercialization of agriculture. The crucial issue of mode of payment to the farmers for their produce on which the present arhtiya system sustains itself is focused upon in Chapter 5. The dependency on arhtiyas increases with the increase in indebtedness, which pushes the farmers toward distressed conditions and sometimes to the extent of taking their own lives. This aspect is explained in Chapter 6. Finally, Chapter 7 of this book brings into focus the main findings, suggestions, and policy alternatives.

In our work, we have received help, support, and feedback from many individuals and organizations. Our gratitude goes to Shri Dipinder Singh, then Secretary, Punjab Mandi Board, for assigning this study, and taking keen interest in this work. We gained much from discussions with Dr R.S. Sidhu, Dr Karam Singh, Dr A.S. Joshi, Dr M.S. Sidhu and H.S. Kingra of Punjab Agricultural University, Ludhiana. Our thanks are due to Ranjana Padhi for her critical comments and suggestions. We place on record our thanks to Dr Harpreet S. Sidhu, S.P. Singh, Kuldip Singh, Amritpal and Sharu Paul for their valuable and timely help.

Last, but not the least, we are thankful to the farmers and arhtiyas for providing us key information that forms the basis of this book.

**Sukhpal Singh**
(sukhpalpau@yahoo.com)

**Tejinder K. Dhaliwal**

# 1

# Origin and Growth of Moneylenders in Punjab

All commerce is based upon money, with moneylending as its integral part, and is one of the oldest professions in the world. It is the single common phenomenon that marks trade and commerce at the local, national, and international levels. In the agrarian economy, too, moneylenders have a long history. Interestingly, in literature, it has been pointed out how everywhere and at all times the moneylender has had a bad name, and some of the most famous figures in history categorically condemned the one thing that sustained moneylending as a trade —the taking of interest in return. Moses, the law-giver of the greatest race of moneylenders in the world, allowed the profession only to one who was not a Jew. In orthodox Islam, it is *haram* (unlawful) to charge interest on a loan. Plato and Aristotle condemned it without even this distinction. In the book, *Politics* by Aristotle, it is said: 'of all modes of making money, this is the most unnatural'. Though the moneylending profession has a long history and was prevalent in all civilizations, its very basis, 'charging interest', was considered unethical, thus making this profession deplorable and disgraceful in society.

## HISTORICAL PERSPECTIVE

To understand how the moneylending system has become so entrenched in Punjab, it is necessary to have a look at its origin and growth. Before the British rule, two castes, namely

*Banias* and *Khatris* (*Aroras*), were involved in the moneylending business in the Punjab province. The strong bonds of village community and social brotherhood were a check on the activities of moneylenders. Moneylenders were always under the social obligation and moral pressure of the rural community. Under British rule, the commercialization of agricultural production and land distorted the rural social set-up; this reduced the authority of the village head body. This body was the main means of checking the exploitative mode and nature of moneylenders. In the 1860s, civil courts were established which legalized the moneylending system. With the establishment of these courts and the decline of the village community, the reign of the moneylenders was fully entrenched in the rural economy. During this period, the moneylending class became very strong and flourished as indebted peasants were compelled to either mortgage or sell their land to them. The peasants were exploited by the British government, landlords, and moneylenders. The British government imposed various types of taxes on peasants and had a limited market system by which the prices of agricultural produce remained very low.

On the other hand, landlords and moneylenders exploited them through usury capital and land transactions. During the last three decades of the nineteenth century, the Punjab province was afflicted with natural disasters like famines, droughts, and mortality of animals due to epidemics, which further deteriorated the economic condition of the already poor peasantry. Thus, the 1870s ushered in an era of peasant indebtedness that had never been witnessed in the region earlier (Thorburn, 1885).

During the late 1890s, the Punjab peasantry faced problems of severe debt and land alienation. To tackle these problems, the British government enacted many laws. In 1901, the Land Alienation Act was passed for preventing the non-agricultural classes from acquiring land from the agriculturists. Similarly, the Cooperative Societies Act was passed in 1904 to solve the problem of rural indebtedness through institutional credit facilities. However, these acts were inadequate to solve the debt problem and to check the process of alienation of peasants from their land. The moneylenders started purchasing land under fictitious names called 'benami'.

The Banking Enquiry Committee was set up in the mid-1920s to assess the magnitude of indebtedness in Punjab. The Royal Commission on agriculture was also formed by the British government in the late 1920s to suggest agrarian reforms and to overcome the agrarian crisis, particularly to jettison the burden of long standing and perpetual indebtedness of the peasantry.

The problem of indebtedness of the Punjab peasantry was highlighted by M.L. Darling in the 1920s, when it was reported that nearly four-fifths of the Punjab peasantry was under debt up to approximately 5 to 6 times their annual income. The total debt of the erstwhile Punjab farmers was Rs. 175 crores, which was 20 per cent of the total debt of the Indian farmers. The interest paid by the farmers of the state amounted to Rs. 50 crores per annum. In this way, private lending became a prosperous business; a large number of people entered into this business. Thus, the proportionate share of moneylenders in the total population of Punjab was five times more than in the rest of the country. The study remarked that, 'the Punjab peasant is born in debt, lives in debt and dies in debt' (Darling, 1925).

Before independence, the British government enacted several laws to regulate the money lending business for united Punjab. The laws include: the Usurious Loans Act 1918, the Provincial Insolvency Act 1920, and long before these laws, the Usury Laws Repeal Act was enacted in 1855.

More legislation was enacted to redress the pathetic situation of the peasantry in the 1930s. These acts were: the

Punjab Regulation of Accounts Act 1930, the Punjab Relief of Indebtedness Act 1934, the Punjab Restitution of Mortgaged Lands Act 1938, the Punjab Alienation of Land (Amendment) Act 1938, and the Punjab Registration of Moneylenders Act 1938. These acts were enacted to systematize the functioning and legitimize the role of agriculturist–moneylenders in the agrarian economy. However, these measures of the British government could not absolve the peasants from the clutches of moneylenders as the magnitude and intensity of farmers debt continuously increased.

The All India Rural Credit Survey (1951–2) revealed that 63 to 78 per cent farm families were indebted and the debt per family was Rs. 744, whereas an average indebted family was under a debt of Rs. 1,137. The average debt per hectare was Rs. 121 and the total debt on Punjab farmers was Rs. 50 crores. This scenario shows that various legislation of the British government led to moneylending business flourishing in the rural economy. As a result, the debt burden of peasantry continued to grow and a large chunk of peasantry was being pushed into the debt trap.

## GREEN REVOLUTION—HIGH DEBT INTENSITY

The green revolution model was introduced in the selective regions of the country during the mid-1960s to solve the agrarian crisis and food shortage. This model was based on a set of measures aimed at technological upgradation of primitive modes of agriculture production along with a set of compatible institutional and policy changes. With the result, the agricultural production process of the state became highly mechanized and capital intensive. Unfortunately, it became unaffordable for the small farmer to transform the traditional agricultural system to the capital intensive one. They had to depend upon other sources of finance for investment in farm structure and agrochemicals. Their owned and borrowed capital investment could not generate sufficient income even for farm expenditure, living expenses, and social festivities. As a result, they got fresh loans at higher rates of interest to pay back the old debts. In this way, the farmers fell into the vicious circle of indebtedness.

The nationalization of banks and the financing of the priority sectors and agriculture within the priority sector provide some solace to the peasantry, which, however, remained short-lived. The All India Debt and Investment Survey (1991–2) showed that 30 per cent of the farmers in Punjab were under debt to the tune of Rs. 7,125 per household. The total debt was estimated to be Rs. 784 crores, out of which the major share came from non-institutional sources (RBI, 1991–2).

In 1997, the total debt on the Punjab farmers was Rs. 5,700 crores and about 89 per cent of the farmers in the state were indebted. Out of the total debt of the farmers, 46.3 per cent was owed to commission agents (Shergill, 1998). Similarly, the study (Sidhu et al, 2000) concluded that, due to the failure of the cotton crop, about 90 per cent of the farmers of the cotton belt were indebted and the average amount of debt was Rs.112,636, out of which 60.50 per cent came from non-institutional sources. Another study (Singh and Toor, 2005) revealed that 78 per cent of farm households were under debt and the debt per household was Rs. 92,394 in 2002–3. The total debt burden on Punjab farmers was estimated at Rs. 9,886 crores out of which 58.1 per cent was from the non-institutional sources.

The National Sample Survey Organisation (NSSO, 2005) found that the Punjab farmers were the most heavily indebted and 65.4 per cent of the farmers were under debt. The indebtedness of Rs. 41,576 per farm household in Punjab was the highest amongst all the states. The share of non-institutional sources was found to be 54 per cent compared with 45 per cent for all India.

Another study (Singh Sukhpal et al, 2007) reported that 89 per cent of the farmers were under debt. The total debt was Rs. 21,064 crores, out of which 38 per cent was from non-institutional sources. The study revealed that debt trap is considered to have emerged primarily due to the strong presence of the non-institutional sources of credit. Some of the farmers even reported that the reason for their indebtedness, was their exploitation by the commission agents[1].

With the mechanization of farm operations, high use of agrochemicals and monoculture cropping system, the demand for human labour in the farm sector has decreased significantly since the late 1980s. For a long time, till the early 1990s, Punjab agriculture had achieved high growth and slowed down thereafter. This happened due to the over exploitation of land and water resources to their harnessing potential. This phenomenon led to increasing costs, a shrinking resource base, declining productivity, falling profitability, and mounting indebtedness. As a result, the de-peasantisation process started in the early 1990s, gained momentum since 2000 as 2 lakh small farmers in the state left farming due to economic distress (Singh Karam et al, 2009). However, the industrial sector in the state could not provide sufficient employment to the labour released from the agriculture sector. Thus, a large chunk of 'reserve army of labour' has been accumulating in the rural economy of the state. The agrarian distress reached a climax by the early 2000s; a study (NSSO, 2005) reported that 40 per cent of the Indian farmers and 37 per cent of the Punjab farmers have

---

[1] The commission agent is a link between the farmers and buyers who in consideration of commission, offers his services to sell agricultural produce in the market. He is also involved in the business of moneylending. He is popularly known as *arhtiya, katcha arhtiya,* or moneylender.

expressed their desire to leave farming as it was no longer an easy and lucrative occupation. Socioeconomic factors like declining profitability, expenditure on social festivities, and exploitation by the non-institutional sources have led to pushing farmers further into the debt trap, many of them even committing suicide. According to the latest survey (PAU, 2009), 2,890 farmers and agricultural labourers have committed suicide in Bathinda and Sangrur districts during 2000–8. Out of these, 66 per cent of the victims have committed suicide due to the heavy debt burden mainly from the commission agents.

Although the Punjab peasantry had been facing the problem of economic hardship and indebtedness before the mid-1960s, the green revolution model has further intensified the problem of indebtedness. The transformation of traditional agriculture towards a modern capital intensive one increased the capital requirements of the farmers which made the farmers dependent upon the credit market. The farmers in general and small farmers in particular borrowed these required funds from institutional and non-institutional sources of finance, especially from commission agents. This process led to an increase in the magnitude of farmers' debt till late 1980s. Even after this period, due to high capital investment and falling net income in agriculture, the magnitude and intensity of farmers' debt increased drastically.

## OBJECTIVES OF THE STUDY

In view of the current agrarian crisis of the state and the role of commission agents, particularly in light of the existing mode of payment of agricultural produce to the farmers, it is important to study the status of the commission agent system in Punjab agriculture in the wake of assured marketing through minimum support price for principal crops and the developed institutional financial market in the state. The relevance of payment for crops to the farmers through middlemen or cheques is an important issue that will help to understand the market imperfections in the state's agriculture. The dominance of commission agents varies zone-wise, as farmers of the south-west zone, in particular, are heavily indebted and severely trapped in the exploitative modus operandi of the commission agents. This increases the significance of studying these variations in different agroclimatic zones and sociocultural zones of the state.

The specific objectives of the study are to:

1. study the role and status of commission agents in the agricultural sector of Punjab State;
2. examine the changing scenario of the commission agent system in the light of socioeconomic characteristics, caste-wise distribution, and traditional and non-traditional classification of commission agents in different zones of the state;
3. know the perceptions of the farmers and the commission agents regarding the commission agent system and the direct payment system to the farmers through cheques for their produce;
4. study the role of commission agents in the context of agrarian distress in Punjab; and
5. spell out the policy implications of the study.

## APPROACH OF THE STUDY

The primary data regarding the commission agent system and the direct payment system in agricultural marketing was collected from the commission agents and the farmers were selected through a random sampling technique. Three different questionnaires were used: one for collecting information from sampled markets, one for the commission agents, and the third for the farmers. The data were collected using the personal interview method during the year 2008—9.

TABLE 1.1: **Sampling Design for Commission Agents in Different Agroclimatic Zones, Punjab**

| *Zone* | *Total Districts* | *Selected Districts* | *Selected Grain Markets* | *Sample Size* | |
|---|---|---|---|---|---|
| | | | | *Commission Agents* | *Farmers* |
| **Sub-mount-ainous (Zone I)** | Rupnagar | Rupnagar | Morinda | 20 | 25 |
| | Hoshiarpur | Hoshiarpur | Tanda Urmur | 20 | 26 |
| | SBS Nagar | - | - | - | - |
| **Subtotal** | **3** | **2** | **2** | **40** | **51** |
| **Central (Zone II)** | Ludhiana | Ludhiana | Khanna | 20 | 27 |
| | Moga | Moga | Moga | 20 | 27 |
| | Barnala | Barnala | Mehal Kalan | 20 | 27 |
| | Fatehgarh Sahib | Fatehgarh Sahib | Khumanoo | 20 | 27 |
| | Jalandhar | Jalandhar | Gorayan | 20 | 26 |
| | Kapurthala | Kapurthala | Phagwara | 20 | 26 |
| | Amritsar | Amritsar | Bhagtanwali | 20 | 26 |
| | Gurdaspur | Gurdaspur | Gurdaspur | 20 | 26 |
| | Sangrur | Sangrur | Bhawanigarh | 20 | 26 |
| | Mohali | - | - | - | - |

| *Zone* | *Total Districts* | *Selected Districts* | *Selected Grain Markets* | *Sample Size* | |
|---|---|---|---|---|---|
| | | | | *Commission Agents* | *Farmers* |
| | Tarn Taran | - | - | - | - |
| | Patiala | - | - | - | - |
| **Subtotal** | **12** | **9** | **9** | **180** | **238** |
| **South-western (Zone III)** | Faridkot | Faridkot | Kotakpura | 20 | 28 |
| | Mukatsar | Mukatsar | Mukatsar | 20 | 28 |
| | Bathinda | Bathinda | Rampura Phul | 20 | 28 |
| | Mansa | Mansa | Mansa | 20 | 27 |
| | Firozpur | - | - | - | - |
| **Subtotal** | **5** | **4** | **4** | **80** | **111** |
| **Total** | **20** | **15** | **15** | **300** | **400** |

The Punjab State is divided into three well-defined agroclimatic zones namely, sub-mountainous zone, central zone, and south-western zone (Table 1.1), which occupy 9 per cent, 65 per cent, and 26 per cent of the net area of the state, respectively. The dominant cropping systems in these zones are maize-wheat, paddy-wheat and cotton-wheat, respectively.

A list of all the grain markets from these three zones was prepared. A total of 15 markets (*mandis*) were selected randomly, choosing 2 from the sub-mountainous zone, 9 from the central zone and 4 from the south-western zone, which is in proportion to the net area sown in each zone.

The cultural stratification of the Punjab State into three cultural zones namely, Majha, Malwa, and Doaba, which also capture some economic stratification due to resource endowment, development, and productivity differentials that developed over time might also have some impact on the farmer-commission agent relationship/exploitations. Thus, the sampling as above was also reclassified into cultural zones (Table 1.2).

One grain market from each selected district was randomly selected. Thereafter, a sample of 20 commission agents from each selected market was randomly taken. In this way, 40 commission agents from the sub-mountainous zone, 180 from the central zone, and 80 from the south-western zone were selected. Thus, a total of 300 commission agents were selected for the study. Similarly, from the sub-mountainous zone 51 farmers, from the central zone 238 farmers, and from the south-western zone 111 farmers were randomly selected. Thus, a total sample of 400 farmers was taken from the adjoining villages of the selected markets for the present study. In this way, a total sample of 700 respondents was taken for the present study.

In order to see the association between two variables, the chi-square test was applied. Similarly, compound growth

TABLE 1.2: **Sampling Design for Commission Agents in Different Cultural Zones, Punjab**

| *Zone* | *Total Districts* | *Selected Districts* | *Selected Grain Markets* | *Sample Size* | |
|---|---|---|---|---|---|
| | | | | *Commission Agents* | *Farmers* |
| **Majha** | Amritsar | Amritsar | Bhagtanwali | 20 | 26 |
| Gurdaspur | Gurdaspur | Gurdaspur | 20 | 26 | |
| Tarn Taran | - | - | - | - | |
| **Subtotal** | **3** | **2** | **2** | **40** | **52** |
| **Malwa** | Barnala | Barnala | Mehal Kalan | 20 | 27 |
| | Ludhiana | Ludhiana | Khanna | 20 | 27 |
| | Moga | Moga | Moga | 20 | 27 |
| | Sangrur | Sangrur | Bhawanigarh | 20 | 26 |
| | Faridkot | Faridkot | Kotakpura | 20 | 28 |
| | Mukatsar | Mukatsar | Mukatsar | 20 | 28 |
| | Bathinda | Bathinda | Rampura Phul | 20 | 28 |
| | Mansa | Mansa | Mansa | 20 | 27 |
| | Firozpur | - | - | - | - |

| *Zone* | *Total Districts* | *Selected Districts* | *Selected Grain Markets* | *Sample Size* | |
|---|---|---|---|---|---|
| | | | | *Commission Agents* | *Farmers* |
| | Fatehgarh Sahib | Fatehgarh Sahib | Khumanoo | 20 | 27 |
| | Mohali | - | - | - | - |
| | Patiala | - | - | - | - |
| **Subtotal** | **12** | **9** | **9** | **180** | **245** |
| **Doaba** | Hoshiarpur | Hoshiarpur | Tanda Urmur | 20 | 26 |
| | Jalandhar | Jalandhar | Gorayan | 20 | 26 |
| | Kapurthala | Kapurthala | Phagwara | 20 | 26 |
| | Rupnagar | Rupnagar | Morinda | 20 | 25 |
| | SBS Nagar | - | - | - | - |
| **Subtotal** | **5** | **4** | **4** | **80** | **103** |
| **Total** | **20** | **15** | **15** | **300** | **400** |

rates (CGR) were computed to work out the trends in time series data.

## CONCEPTS USED

*i.* ***Arhat:*** An amount paid to the middleman/commission agent for his services for marketing the agricultural produce is called arhat. The arhat and commission are synonymous terms.

*ii.* **Katcha Arhtiya:** Katcha arhtiya means a dealer who, for a consideration of commission, offers his services to sell agricultural produce. Katcha arhtiyas are also known as commission agents or arhtiyas.

*iii.* ***Pucca* Arhtiya:** Pucca arhtiya means a dealer, who for himself or on behalf of any other person, makes or offers to make a purchase or sale of any agricultural produce or does or offers to do anything for carrying out such purchase or sale.

*iv.* **Traditional Commission Agents:** The commission agent families engaged in the business of arhat or commission agent from before the green revolution (mid-1960s), are considered as traditional commission agents.

*v.* **Non-traditional Commission Agents:** The families who joined the arhat or commission agent business after the initiation of the green revolution (mid-1960s), are considered as non-traditional commission agents.

*vi.* ***Damami*:** An amount of commission which the commission agent deducts from the farmer in case of low market arrival, either due to low productivity or crop failure, is called damami. In this practice, the commission agent charges commission from the farmers equivalent to the previous years' commission.

*vii.* **J-Form:** The commission agent issues a J-Form to the farmers (seller), after the procurement of the crop. In this form, the name of the seller, buyer, and arhtiya is written. The name and volume of produce sold, the rate, the amount of the produce, the incidental charges, and the net amount paid to the farmers is also included in this form. In the case of vegetables and fruits, the name of the buyer is not necessary to write in the J-Form. The issuance of a J-Form by the commission agent to the farmers is mandatory.

*viii.* **I- Form:** The commission agent issues an I-Form to the buyer of the produce. In the I-Form, the details of commodity purchased are given. The name of the commodity, volume, rate, total amount, and market charges including commission, brokerage, *palledari*, filling, sewing, and other charges are given. The issuance of the I-Form by the commission agent to the buyer is mandatory.

*ix.* **Green Revolution and Post-Green Revolution Period:** The green revolution period indicates the period from the mid-1960s to the late 1980s whereas the period since early 1990s has been considered as the post-green revolution period.

# 2

# Status of the Commission Agent Stystem in Punjab Agriculture

The commission agent, particularly known as arhtiya, is the most dominant person in the agricultural marketing system of the state. Traditionally, commission agents have emerged from petty shopkeepers and merchants. They provide domestic consumable articles on credit and are also involved in the activity of moneylending. Trading in agricultural produce brought them close to peasants and the wholesale traders. They perform the function of becoming a link between the farmers (sellers) and buyers (consumers, wholesalers, procurement agencies, et cetera) for facilitating the auction and delivery of the produce to the buyers. They arrange payment for the farmers (sellers) and other facilities like loading/unloading and cleaning of the produce. They also make arrangements for the required equipment and machines for weighing, filling, and stitching the grain bags, though the farmers and buyers pay for these services according to the rates prescribed by the Punjab Mandi Board as per the Punjab Agricultural Produce Market Act, 1961. The commission agent issues the J-Form to the farmers (Appendix I) and I-Form to the buyer of the produce (Appendix II). The commission agents also provide the agricultural inputs, domestic articles, and money to the farmers.

The commission agent is a link between sellers and buyers, apart from acting as a moneylender in agriculture marketing. Here emerges the need and methodology of how the commission agent system actually works in the rural lending market. The commission agent lends the money to the farmers during the period when crops are growing in the fields, when farmers need the money and the marketing season is very brisk, that is, when commission agents need little money in their own businesses. Then the commission agents recover their money when the farmer markets his produce, that is, when the commission agents need money for their businesses. In theory, this system seems perfect, but in practice, this mechanism has so many inbuilt loopholes through which the commission agents indulge in malpractices often culminating into overindulgence in exploitation realizing that the farmers, particularly the smaller ones, are the weaker party. Often, they come to deduct their loaned money even before the farmer is left with any surplus to meet his emergency or current needs. In this practice, the commission agent exploits the farmer in double shifts, that is, not only when the farmer is with him as a seller but also when the farmer is forced to remain with him as a buyer for his domestic and farm needs. The major source of exploitation is the cash in the hand of the commission agent before the payment to the farmer for his produce.

The relationship between commission agents and farmers has remained a vexed one. It is being reported more in the recent past, that the farmers are being increasingly exploited through all these transactions, especially with the worsening of the agrarian crisis. Commission agents exploit the farmers by charging an exorbitant rate of interest, supplying spurious farm inputs, and through other various malpractices in marketing activities.

Keeping in view the increasingly exploitative network of commission agents, some academicians and policy makers have strongly suggested reducing the role of market intermediaries and regulating the commission agent system in the agricultural sector.

The report of the expert committee on 'Possibility to Reduce the Number of Intermediaries in Agricultural Marketing System in the State of Punjab', submitted to Government of Punjab in 1998, strongly recommended the reduction in the number of middlemen/intermediaries. The committee suggested that the procurement agencies should directly purchase the farmers' produce at their stores/ godowns without the help of commission agents. The committee also stressed that the Punjab Mandi Board and market committee should continue to provide better facilities and infrastructure to reduce the dependence on middlemen, which would be in the long-term interest of the farm economy of the state (GoP, 1998).

A study done in 2005 (Rangi & Sidhu, 2005) revealed that almost all the commission agents in agricultural marketing have their own shops in the regulated markets and about 30 per cent of them have allied businesses. Almost all these occupations are related to the farm sector. The commission agent supplies farm inputs to farmers on a credit basis and provides loans on which he charges a high rate of interest. He does not issue J-Forms to 44 per cent of the farmers. The study also reported cases of commission agents purchasing agricultural land belonging to farmers.

Another study jointly conducted by Punjab Agricultural University, Ludhiana and the Punjab State Farmers Commission reveals that the farmers of Punjab State are heavily indebted due to, amongst other reasons, the strong presence of non-institutional sources, particularly commission agents in the state. The study explored and commented that the proper records of non-institutional sources of finance are not maintained and many times these loans are over-charged because of farmers' illiteracy. Farmers are also exploited by charging a high rate of interest which varies between 24 to 36 per cent. The dependence of small and marginal farmers on non-institutional loans is high, exposing them to the unscrupulous operations of non-institutional credit agencies, especially commission agents and other moneylenders. The activities of non-institutional sources of credit are not regulated. The commission agent exploits the farmers not only by charging an exorbitant rate of interest but also by supplying all types of farm inputs and domestic articles from their own or linked shops, thereby increasing the indebtedness of the dependent farmer. Thus, they have developed full control over the agricultural market in the state. They deduct their loans even before making the payments for the produce marketed by the farmers. It is therefore important that the government should exercise a strong check on their activities. In a nutshell, the government should regularize and continuously monitor the functioning of the non-institutional sources of finance to ensure a fair deal to the farmers. In particular, the payment to the farmers should be made through cheques so that the farmers come out of the clutches of bonded financial markets of arhtiyas (Singh Sukhpal et al, 2007). These reports show the gravity of the prevailing commission agent system in the overall context of the agrarian crisis in Punjab.

## I. STRENGTH OF COMMISSION AGENTS IN PUNJAB AGRICULTURE

The magnitude of commission agents can be seen from the number of licenses issued to the commission agents and the number of commission agent families who are engaged in this profession.

### 1. Magnitude of Licenses of Commission Agents

Punjab Mandi Board issued a total number of 37,506 licenses of commission agents for different markets in the state (Table 2.1). However, there are 4,535 *pucca* arhtiya licensees in different markets of the state (Appendix III). Basically these persons are dealers who can make the purchase or sale of any agricultural produce. The zone-wise picture of commission agents (katcha arhtiyas) in grain markets depicts that it is the highest in zone II (20,078) followed by zone III (12,620) and zone I (1,277). Similarly, the total number of commission agent licenses for fruits and vegetables are 2,933 in the state. These licenses are the highest in zone II (2,286), followed by zone I (359) and, Zone III (288). As the farmers of the state are mainly engaged in the cultivation of wheat, paddy, and cotton, the number of commission agent licenses for the grain markets is the highest (33,975), followed by the number of commission agent licenses for the fruits and vegetables (2,933), wood market (565), and wheat straw market (33). The commission agents who are dealing with grain marketing have a direct relationship with a large section of peasantry as the commission agents are involved in the production, consumption of crops, and sociopolitical dimensions of peasantry. Keeping in view the present scenario of crop farming and the nature and relationship of peasantry in the state, the present study is concerned mainly with the commission agents who are dealing with the grain markets.

TABLE 2.1: **District-wise Number of Commission Agent Licensees for Different Markets in Punjab**

| *Zone* | *District* | *Grain Market* | *Fruits & Vegetable Market* | *Wood Market* | *Wheat Straw Market* | *Total* |
|---|---|---|---|---|---|---|
| I | Rupnagar | 227 | 64 | 44 | 3 | 338 |
| | Hoshiarpur | 555 | 273 | 37 | - | 865 |
| | SBS Nagar | 495 | 22 | 49 | - | 566 |
| | **Subtotal** | **1277** | **359** | **130** | **3** | **1769** |
| II | Patiala | 2451 | 344 | 34 | 4 | 2833 |
| | Jalandhar | 1122 | 126 | 6 | 2 | 1256 |
| | Ludhiana | 2226 | 518 | 35 | 3 | 2782 |

| Zone | District | Grain Market | Fruits & Vegetable Market | Wood Market | Wheat Straw Market | Total |
|---|---|---|---|---|---|---|
| | Fatehgarh Sahib | 649 | 31 | 30 | - | 710 |
| | Barnala | 1552 | 5 | 9 | - | 1566 |
| | Sangrur | 3275 | 135 | 21 | - | 3431 |
| | Gurdaspur | 1484 | 234 | 16 | - | 1734 |
| | Moga | 2498 | 79 | 3 | 4 | 2584 |
| | Mohali | 147 | 107 | 82 | 17 | 253 |
| | Kapurthala | 921 | 98 | 14 | - | 1033 |
| | Amritsar | 2000 | 547 | 72 | - | 2619 |
| | Tarn Taran | 1753 | 62 | 16 | - | 1831 |
| | **Subtotal** | **20078** | **2286** | **338** | **30** | **22732** |
| III | Firozpur | 3652 | 144 | 1 | - | 3797 |
| | Faridkot | 1455 | 61 | 58 | - | 1574 |
| | Mukatsar | 2090 | 39 | 8 | - | 2137 |
| | Bathinda | 2757 | - | 20 | | 2777 |
| | Mansa | 2666 | 44 | 10 | - | 2720 |
| **Subtotal** | | **12620** | **288** | **97** | **-** | **13005** |
| **Total** | | **33975** | **2933** | **565** | **33** | **37506** |

## 2. Magnitude of Commission Agent Families

Punjab state has well-diversified agricultural markets. There are 145 regulated markets in the state, out of which 12 fall in zone I, 100 in zone II and, 33 markets fall in zone III (Table 2.2). Similarly, there is a vast net work of 294 sub-yards for the marketing of agricultural produce.

The total number of commission agent families working in the grain markets in the state is 20,232 (Table 2.2; Figure I). It is the general perception of the people that the magnitude and intensity of commission agent families varies in the different agroclimatic zones of the state. The number of these families is the highest in zone II (13,752), followed by zone III (5,416), and lastly zone I (1,064). The families of commission agents engaged in the profession are far less than the number of licenses due to the issuance and existence of multiple licenses and inoperative licenses.

Average number of licenses per commission agent family is 1.66 in the state, which is the highest in zone III (2.33), followed by zone II (1.46), and zone I (1.20). The number of commission agents per thousand hectares of net area sown is 4.84 in the state. This number is the highest in zone II (5.06), followed by zone III (4.98) and zone I (2.83). Similarly, the average number of commission agents is 20.29 for one thousand farmer families in the state. This number is the highest in zone III (23.15), followed by zone II (22.36) and zone I (7.19).

TABLE 2.2: **Concentration of Commission Agent Families in Grain Markets of Punjab**

| *Zone* | *Total families of commission agents** | *Net area sown (000,ha)* | *Total number of regulated markets* | *Total number of sub-yards* | *No. of farmer households (000)* | *Concentration of commission agents* | | *Average number of licenses per commission agent family* |
|---|---|---|---|---|---|---|---|---|
| | | | | | | *Per 000, ha net area sown* | *Per 000, farm families* | |
| I | 1064 | 376 | 12 | 27 | 148 | 2.83 | 7.19 | 1.20 |
| II | 13752 | 2720 | 100 | 194 | 615 | 5.06 | 22.36 | 1.46 |
| III | 5416 | 1088 | 33 | 73 | 234 | 4.98 | 23.15 | 2.33 |
| **Punjab** | 20232 | 4184 | 145 | 294 | 997 | 4.84 | 20.29 | 1.66 |

*Estimated on the basis of number of commission agent families in the sampled markets

This analysis reveals that the concentration of commission agents is the lowest in zone I of the state. The reason behind this phenomenon is the comparatively higher level of education, more foreign migration, and less commercial farming in this zone.

## II. COMMISSION OR ARHAT OF COMMISSION AGENTS

The commission agents, popularly known as arhtiyas, had a long history in the agrarian economy of the state. Before the green revolution, their role was limited to moneylending but during the post-green revolution period, their mode of functioning and status has changed significantly. Being middlemen in agricultural marketing, commission agents charge commission from the buyers. On the basis of the Punjab Agricultural Produce Markets Act, 1961, the Punjab Mandi Board had fixed their commission for different crops, including fruits and vegetables. The rate of commission was fixed at the rate of 1.50 per cent of the value of farm produce on 26 May 1961 on *ad valurem* basis. However, commission agents being a strong lobby politically, could manage to increase their commission from time to time with their continuous pressure on the state government (Table 2.3).

TABLE 2.3: **Changes in the Rate of Commission Paid to Commission Agents in Punjab**

| *Period* | | *Commission @* | *Basis* |
|---|---|---|---|
| *From* | *To* | | |
| 26-05-1961 | 10-04-1990 | 1.50% | ad valurem |
| 11-04-1990 | 21-05-1998 | 2.00% | ad valurem |
| 22-05-1998 | Till date | 2.50% | ad valurem |

The rate of commission was raised to 2.00 per cent on 11 April 1990 and on 22 May 1998, the commission was again raised to 2.50 per cent on all agricultural commodities, except fruits and vegetables.

Table 2.4 reveals the present market charges and commission of commission agents for the procurement of different agricultural commodities. On foodgrains and cotton, this commission is 2.5 per cent of the value of the produce.

TABLE 2.4: **Market Charges Levied in Punjab, 2009–10**

| *Description* | *Produce* | *Charges on ad valorem basis (%)* |
|---|---|---|
| Commission of the Arhtiya | Foodgrains, Cotton | 2.5 |
| | Fruit &Vegetables | 5 |
| | Chillies | 1.5 |
| Infrastructure cess | Wheat, Paddy | 3 |
| | Cotton | 2 |
| Market fee | All crops | 2 |
| Rural development fund | All crops | 2 |
| Sale/Purchase Tax | All crops | 4 |

Note: On purchase of cotton by the mega projects, there is no infrastructure cess.

This rate is very high, to the extent of 5 per cent for the sale of fruits and vegetables. However, for chillies, it is comparatively low at 1.5 per cent. The market charges have been the highest in Punjab for long. At present, the total market charges are 13.5 per cent of the value of the produce; this constitutes 4 per cent as purchase tax, 3 per cent as the infrastructure cess on wheat and paddy where it is 2 per cent in the case of cotton, 2 per cent as market fee, 2 per cent as the rural development fund, and 2.5 per cent as the arhat (commission) for the commission agents.

It is a well known fact that the agriculture of the state was diversified in the pre-green revolution period; now the cropping system is confined to wheat, paddy, and cotton crops only, which cover about 85 per cent of the total crop area of the state. It is pertinent to note that a minimum support price mechanism is effectively working for wheat and paddy crops in the state as the public procurement agencies purchase these crops without any useful involvement of middlemen. In this context, it is relevant to calculate the amount of commission paid to commission agents by public procurement agencies.

Thus, in the present report, we have tried to calculate the commission paid to commission agents on the basis of market fee charges only on the three crops, namely wheat, paddy, and cotton. On the procurement of wheat, paddy, and cotton during 1961 to 1990, the rate of commission was fixed at the rate of 1.50 per cent of the value of produce sold in the market. In this way, the commission agents had got Rs. 15.56 crores and Rs. 15.66 crores from wheat and paddy crops respectively during 1985–6 (Table 2.5; Figure II). The amount of this commission has continuously increased with minor fluctuations as the market arrival and prices of these crops have increased over a period of time.

However, the spectacular increase in the commission amount has been witnessed after the increase in the rate of commission in 1990 from 1.5 per cent to 2.0 per cent and further from 2.0 per cent to 2.5 per cent in 1998. As a result, the amount of commission from wheat and paddy crops increased from Rs. 26.98 crores and Rs. 33.29 crores to Rs. 30.15 crores and Rs. 35.45 crores from wheat and paddy crops respectively during 1989–90 to 1990–1 and further from Rs. 72.60 crores and 112.08 crores to 109.19 and 143.76 crores from wheat and paddy crops respectively during 1998–9 to 1999–2000.

TABLE 2.5: **Commission Charged by the Commission Agents on Wheat, Paddy and Cotton in Punjab**(Rs. crores)

| *Year* | *Wheat* | | *Paddy* | | *Cotton* | |
|---|---|---|---|---|---|---|
| | *Market fee* | *Commi-ssion commi-ssion agent* | *Market fee* | *Commi-ssion to commi-ssion agent* | *Market fee* | *Commi-ssion to commi-ssion agent* |
| 1985–6 | 20.69 | 15.56 | 20.83 | 15.66 | 5.64 | 4.24 |
| 1986–7 | 22.32 | 16.78 | 22.73 | 17.09 | 7.70 | 5.79 |
| 1987–8 | 16.37 | 12.31 | 24.82 | 18.66 | 11.20 | 8.42 |
| 1988–9 | 19.95 | 15.00 | 22.93 | 17.24 | 16.15 | 12.14 |
| 1989–90 | 26.98 | 26.98 | 33.29 | 33.29 | 13.44 | 13.44 |
| 1990–1 | 30.15 | 30.15 | 35.45 | 35.45 | 18.40 | 18.40 |
| 1991–2 | 29.74 | 29.74 | 40.44 | 40.44 | 25.78 | 25.78 |
| 1992–3 | 30.50 | 30.50 | 47.46 | 47.46 | 24.13 | 24.13 |
| 1993–4 | 42.60 | 42.60 | 62.75 | 62.75 | 21.90 | 21.90 |
| 1994–5 | 52.69 | 52.69 | 69.08 | 69.08 | 25.64 | 25.64 |
| 1995–6 | 53.77 | 53.77 | 55.75 | 55.75 | 24.13 | 24.13 |
| 1996–7 | 45.70 | 45.70 | 65.55 | 65.55 | 27.49 | 27.49 |
| 1997–8 | 54.92 | 54.92 | 88.74 | 88.74 | 13.93 | 13.93 |
| 1998–9 | 58.08 | 72.60 | 89.66 | 112.08 | 9.38 | 11.73 |
| 1999–2000 | 87.35 | 109.19 | 115.01 | 143.76 | 11.79 | 14.74 |
| 2000–1 | 113.70 | 142.13 | 124.33 | 155.41 | 15.78 | 19.73 |
| 2001–2 | 129.25 | 161.56 | 134.19 | 167.74 | 14.15 | 17.69 |
| 2002–3 | 122.74 | 153.43 | 151.05 | 188.81 | 13.40 | 16.75 |
| 2003–4 | 111.03 | 138.79 | 173.52 | 216.90 | 23.53 | 29.41 |
| 2004–5 | 117.43 | 146.79 | 185.51 | 231.89 | 28.37 | 35.46 |
| 2005–6 | 115.64 | 144.55 | 179.47 | 224.34 | 35.96 | 44.95 |
| 2006–7 | 101.32 | 126.65 | 171.37 | 214.21 | 42.83 | 53.54 |
| 2007–8 | 111.60 | 139.50 | 192.52 | 240.65 | 44.97 | 56.21 |
| 2008–9 | 205.06 | 256.33 | 295.46 | 369.33 | 39.35 | 49.19 |
| 2009–10 (Provisional) | 237.65 | 297.06 | 344.79 | 430.99 | 41.40 | 51.75 |

*From 1985–6 to 1988–9, the charges are estimated on the basis of market arrivals.

**Figure I: Commission Charged by the Commission Agents on Wheat, Paddy and Cotton in Punjab**

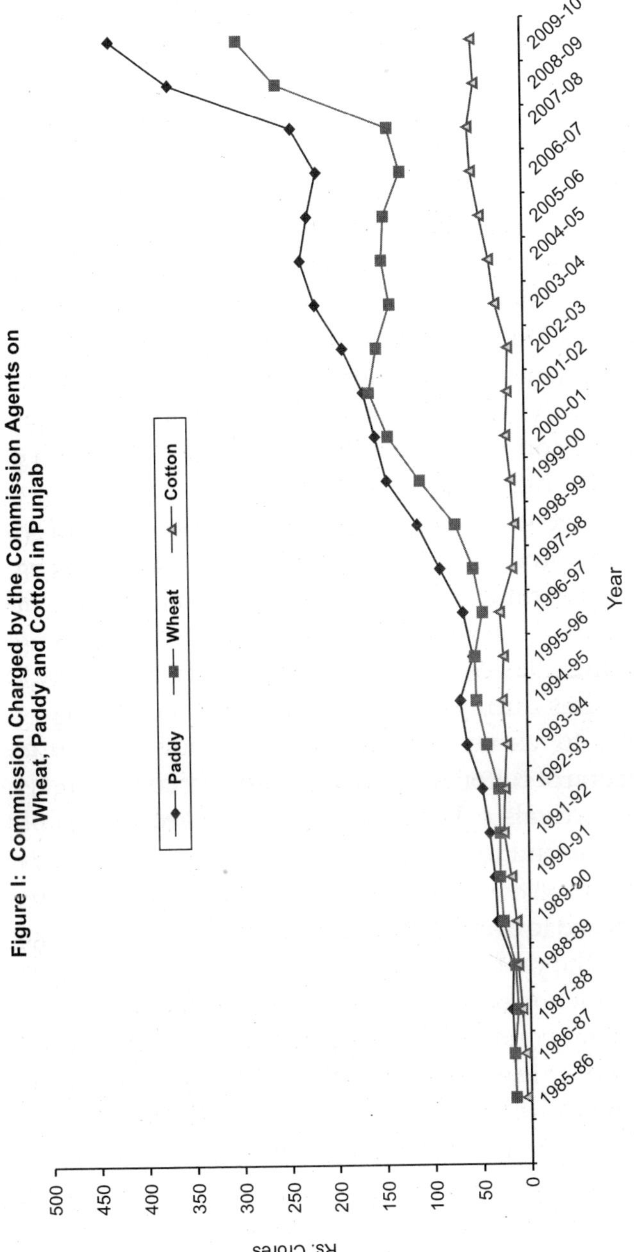

Thus, it can be safely concluded that in an overall sense, the amount of commission has increased over time. Commission agents have earned a sum of Rs. 297 crores from wheat and Rs. 431 crores from paddy during the year 2009–10. This amount has increased due to an increase in market arrivals, increase in prices of crops, and an increase in the rate of commission on the purchase of these crops.

Cotton crop, popularly known as 'white gold', has remained gold not only for farmers but also for market intermediaries. Due to an ineffective minimum support price of cotton, farmers are sometimes exploited by the private traders. Similarly, due to a lack of specific quality parameters in the case of cotton crops, farmers had in some cases, got lower prices which lowered the amount of commission to commission agents. The commission paid to the commission agents on the procurement of the cotton crop has increased over a period of time, though with some fluctuations. It was Rs. 4.24 crores in the year 1985–6 and increased to Rs. 13.44 crores during 1989–90. This amount further increased to Rs. 18.40 crores during 1990–1 and Rs. 27.49 crores during 1996–7. Due to a severe attack of the American bollworm, the production of cotton reached its lowest ebb; consequently, the market arrivals of the cotton crop declined drastically from 851 thousand tonnes to 231 thousand tonnes from the year 1996–7 to 1998–9. As a result, the amount of commission fell and reached to even less than half (Rs. 11.73 crores) during 1998–9 from the year 1996–7 (Rs. 27.49 crores). However, due to the introduction of new varieties of cotton and favourable environmental conditions, the production of cotton in the state started gaining ground; thus the commission for middlemen has also started increasing since 2000.

On the procurement of all the commodities, the market fee and commission charged by commission agents is given in Table 2.6 and depicted through Figure III.

TABLE 2.6: **Commission Charged by the Commission Agents on Fruits & Vegetables and All Commodities in Punjab**

| *Year* | *Total all commodities (Rs. Crores)* | |
|---|---|---|
| | *Market fee* | *Commission to commission Agent* |
| 1989–90 | 80.88 | 96.34 |
| 1990–1 | 92.78 | 109.71 |
| 1991–2 | 105.37 | 124.71 |
| 1992–3 | 114.53 | 135.80 |
| 1993–4 | 138.81 | 164.41 |
| 1994–5 | 161.46 | 192.10 |
| 1995–6 | 146.56 | 172.78 |
| 1996–7 | 153.76 | 180.83 |
| 1997–8 | 174.60 | 204.73 |
| 1998–9 | 175.74 | 203.20 |
| 1999–2000 | 231.42 | 272.01 |
| 2000–1 | 270.20 | 319.45 |
| 2001–2 | 295.99 | 349.88 |
| 2002–3 | 308.09 | 361.84 |
| 2003–4 | 329.83 | 388.13 |
| 2004–5 | 353.10 | 416.65 |
| 2005–6 | 362.30 | 417.34 |
| 2006–7 | 345.39 | 396.09 |
| 2007–8 | 398.73 | 461.08 |
| 2008–9 | 573.00 | 677.10 |
| 2009–10 | 653.11 | 783.29 |
| Total | 5465.65 | 6427.47 |
| **Average** | **260.27** | **306.07** |

**Figure II: Commission Charged by the Commission Agents on all Commodities in Punjab**

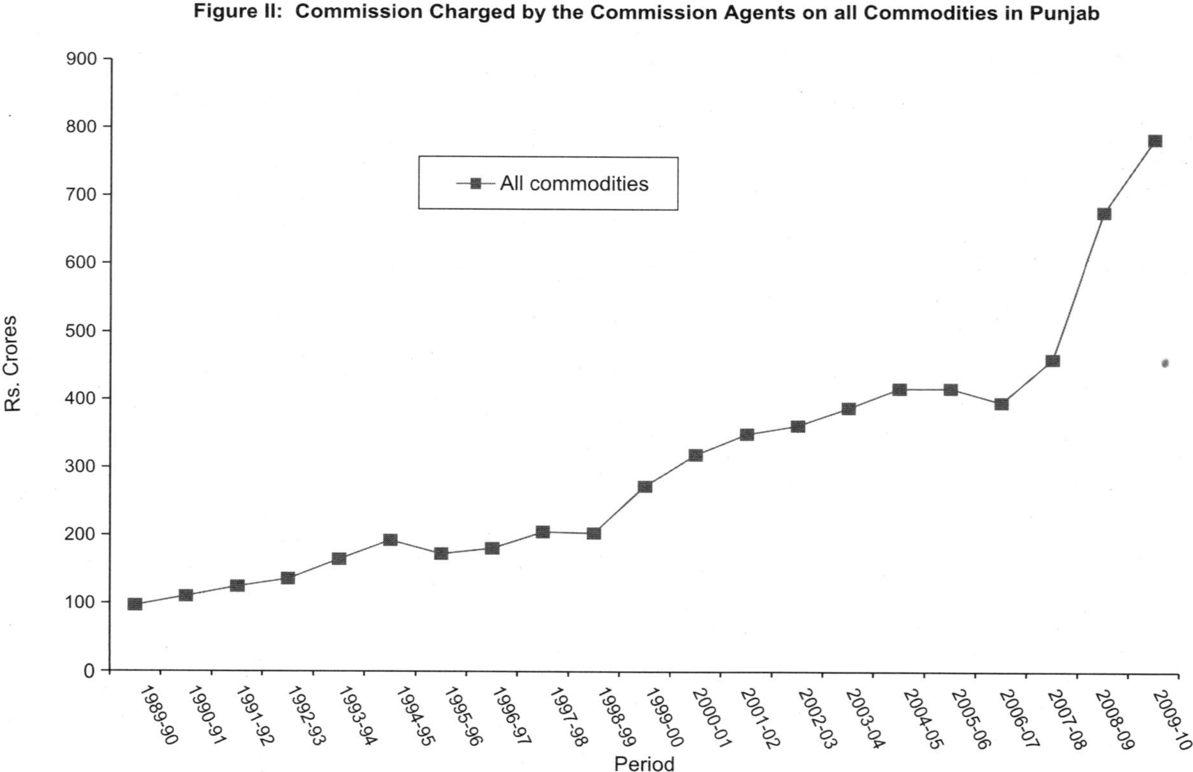

The commission charged by commission agents on all the commodities was Rs. 96.34 crores in 1989–90. Due to the increase in the rate of commission from 1.5 per to 2.0 per cent on 11 April 1990, the amount of commission increased to Rs. 109.71 crores (13.88%) in the next year that is, 1990–1. This amount had been increasing continuously till 1997–8. Thereafter, an abrupt increase in commission has been noticed, as the figure suddenly becomes Rs. 272 crores from Rs. 203 crores in just one year. The hike in this amount was due to an increase in market arrivals, prices of these crops, and ultimately due to the increase in the rate of commission paid to the commission agents. On the whole, it can be concluded that commission agents have earned about Rs. 677 crores during 2008–9 and Rs. 783.29 crores during 2009–10. This amount has increased about eight times from 1989–90 to 2009–10. The rate of growth of the total amount of commission paid to the commission agents from 1989–90 to 2009–10 was 9.74 per cent. On an average, the commission agents earned commission amounting to Rs. 306.07 crores per annum since 1989–90.

Despite the fact that commission agents do not have any significant role in the procurement of those crops (wheat and paddy) in which assured marketing prevails, they are able to increase their commission from time to time. This could be happening on account of the continuous pressure from this lobby; otherwise there is no rationale for such an increase in their commission, which was and remains fixed on *ad valurem* basis. As the value of produce increases over a period of time and the market arrivals and prices increase every year, the arhtiyas' commission automatically increases. Whether this happens for the services of commission agents or it is their manipulation for the exploitation of the state exchequer, is open to speculation.

## III. SOCIOECONOMIC CHARACTERISTICS OF COMMISSION AGENTS

The sampled commission agents have been segregated on the basis of their age, education level and caste.

### 1. Age and Education Level of Commission Agents

The majority of the commission agents (59%) fall in the age group of 31 to 50 years and only 7.33 per cent were found to be below 30 years (Table 2.7). Education level indicates that 37 per cent of the commission agents are graduates and only 7 per cent are below matric level of education.

TABLE 2.7: **Age and Education Level of Commission Agents in Punjab**

| *Characteristics* | *Number of Commission Agents* | *Percentage* |
|---|---|---|
| **(a) Age (years)** | | |
| ≤ 30 | 22 | 7.33 |
| 31-40 | 79 | 26.33 |
| 41-50 | 98 | 32.67 |
| >50 | 101 | 33.67 |
| **(b) Education level** | | |
| Illiterate | 5 | 1.67 |
| Primary | 3 | 1.00 |
| Middle | 13 | 4.33 |
| Matric | 103 | 34.33 |
| 10+2 | 58 | 19.33 |
| Graduate | 111 | 37.00 |
| Postgraduate | 7 | 2.33 |

It is very interesting to note that 1.67 per cent of commission agents do not have any formal education, though they know their traditional language, *lande* (codified language). It is a general perception of people that commission agents exploit the farmers through maintaining their accounts in their own language, which nobody can decode nor understand. It is written in such a manner that it can be read only by the person who writes it. So, at the time of maintaining and clearing accounts, not only illiterate farmers but sometimes well educated people are also exploited easily. On the other hand, it is also observed that 2.33 per cent of commission agents have postgraduation qualification.

To get deeper information about social characteristics of the commission agents such as the age and education level, analysis has been done for different agroclimatic zones of the state (Table 2.8). So far as the age of commission agents is concerned, the relative proportion of the younger (≤ 30 years of age) agents is higher (10%) in zone III as compared to that of other zones. Similarly, the proportion of persons between the age group of 31 to 40 years is higher in zone II (31.11%) followed by zone III with 20 per cent and zone I with 17.50 per cent.

TABLE 2.8: **Age and Education Level of Commission Agents in Punjab (Agroclimatic Zone-wise)**

| *Characteristics* | *Zone I* | | *Zone II* | | *Zone III* | |
|---|---|---|---|---|---|---|
| | *Number of Commission Agents* | *%* | *Number of Commission Agents* | *%* | *Number of Commission Agents* | *%* |
| **(a) Age (years)** | | | | | | |
| ≤ 30 | 3 | 7.50 | 11 | 6.11 | 8 | 10.00 |
| 31-40 | 7 | 17.50 | 56 | 31.11 | 16 | 20.00 |
| 41-50 | 13 | 32.50 | 58 | 32.22 | 27 | 33.75 |
| >51 | 17 | 42.50 | 55 | 30.56 | 29 | 36.25 |
| **(b) Education Level** | | | | | | |
| Illiterate | 0 | 0.00 | 3 | 1.67 | 2 | 2.50 |
| Primary | 1 | 2.50 | 2 | 1.11 | 0 | 0.00 |
| Middle | 1 | 2.50 | 5 | 2.78 | 7 | 8.75 |
| Matric | 13 | 32.50 | 60 | 33.33 | 30 | 37.50 |
| 10+2 | 11 | 27.50 | 38 | 21.11 | 9 | 11.25 |
| Graduate | 14 | 35.00 | 69 | 38.33 | 29 | 36.25 |
| Postgraduate | 0 | 0.00 | 3 | 1.67 | 3 | 3.75 |

The education level of commission agents also differs in different agroclimatic zones. In zone I, no illiterate or postgraduate person could be found in this business. On the other hand, the proportion of commission agents who do not have any formal qualification is 1.67 in zone II and 2.50 in zone III. Similarly, there are some commission agents in these zones who are well educated, even upto the postgraduation level. The proportion of graduate commission agents is high in all the zones. It is the highest (38.33%) in zone II, followed by zone III (36.25%), and zone I (35%).

The proportion of the younger commission agents

(≤ 30 years of age) is high in Malwa (8.89%), followed by Doaba (6.25%) and Majha (2.50 %) (Table 2.9). Majha has a higher proportion of middle aged (41–50 years) commission agents with 42.50 per cent, whereas, Malwa and Doaba have a higher proportion of commission agents who have attained the age of more than 50 years.

TABLE 2.9: **Age and Education Level of Commission Agents in Punjab (Cultural Zone-wise)**

| *Characteristics* | *Majha* Number of Commission Agents | % | *Malwa* Number of Commission Agents | % | *Doaba* Number of Commission Agents | % |
|---|---|---|---|---|---|---|
| **(a) Age (years)** | | | | | | |
| ≤ 30 | 1 | 2.50 | 16 | 8.89 | 5 | 6.25 |
| 31-40 | 16 | 40.0 | 47 | 26.11 | 16 | 20.00 |
| 41-50 | 17 | 42.50 | 57 | 31.67 | 24 | 30.00 |
| > 51 | 6 | 15.00 | 60 | 33.33 | 35 | 43.75 |
| **(b) Education level** | | | | | | |
| Illiterate | 1 | 2.50 | 4 | 2.22 | 0 | 0.00 |
| Primary | 0 | 0.00 | 2 | 1.11 | 1 | 1.25 |
| Middle | 1 | 2.50 | 8 | 4.44 | 4 | 5.00 |
| Matric | 10 | 25.00 | 61 | 33.89 | 32 | 40.00 |
| 10+2 | 11 | 27.50 | 30 | 16.67 | 17 | 21.25 |
| Graduate | 17 | 42.50 | 70 | 38.89 | 24 | 30.00 |
| Postgraduate | 0 | 0.00 | 5 | 2.78 | 2 | 2.50 |

The education level of commission agents in different cultural zones of the state is quite different. No illiterate commission agent among sampled respondents is found in the Doaba zone, whereas the proportion of uneducated persons is 2.50 for Majha and 2.22 for the Malwa zone of the state. The proportion of matriculate commission agents is high in the Doaba zone whereas the Majha and Malwa zones have the highest proportion of graduate commission agents.

On the whole, it can be concluded that the proportion of commission agents who had education after matriculation is the highest in Majha zone (70%), followed by Malwa (58.34%) and Doaba zone (53.75%) of the state.

## 2. Caste-wise Distribution of Commission Agents

Traditionally, two castes, namely Banias and Khatris (Aroras), have dominated this business. The nature and behaviour of the Bania caste is unique and they are known for their business qualities. M.L. Darling has described the nature and activities of Bania commission agents as follows:

> The members of Bania caste are so subtle and skilful in this trade that they could give lessons to the most cunning Jews. They accustom their children at an early age to shun slothfulness and instead of letting them go into the streets to lose their time at play, teach them arithmetic which they learn perfectly, using for it neither pen nor counters, but the money alone, so that in a moment they will do a sum, howsoever difficult it may be. If anyone gets into a rage with them they listen with patience without replying anything, and they withdraw coldly, not returning to see him for four or five days, when they believe his rage to be over (Darling 1925).

Presently, however, this business is not confined to these two castes only. Although the dominant caste in this business is still Banias, some new castes have entered the profession. It is a well known fact that the benefits of the green revolution were confined only to those farmers who had sufficient land and owned capital funds, and ultimately, a large volume of marketable surplus. Certainly, large farmers could reap more benefits of this highly capital intensive agriculture. These large farmers have benefited from commercial farming; the profit has been invested either in the farm sector as in land improvement, farming structure, mechanization, or in other sectors of the economy. As a result, some of these large farmers have started their own commission agent business in the state. The entry of these non-traditional commission agents started in the mid-1980s when the green revolution had been passing through the phase of increasing productivity and high profitability.

In Punjab, 35 per cent of commission agents are Banias, about 27 per cent belong to the Jat caste, and 25 per cent belong to the Khatri caste. However, commission agents from some other castes like *Brahmin, Rajput, Kamboj,* and *Saini* are also involved in this business (Table 2.10; Figure IV). This analysis reveals that the capitalist development in agriculture has transformed the rigid caste-based arhtiya system to an economic or business profession.

TABLE 2.10: **Caste-wise Distribution of Commission Agents in Punjab**

| *Caste* | *Number of Commission Agents* | *Percentage* |
|---|---|---|
| Bania | 105 | 35.00 |
| Jat | 80 | 26.67 |
| Khatri | 75 | 25.00 |
| Brahmin | 23 | 7.67 |
| Rajput | 7 | 2.33 |
| Saini | 3 | 1.00 |
| Kamboj | 2 | 0.67 |
| Others* | 5 | 1.67 |
| **Total** | **300** | **100.00** |

* Others include Sonar, Ramgharia, and Labana

The caste-wise distribution of commission agents across different agroclimatic zones (Table 2.11) shows that whereas

**Figure III : Caste-wise Distribution of Commission Agents, Punjab**

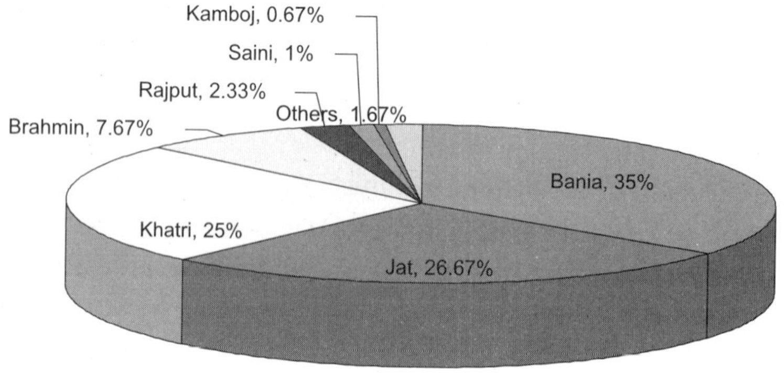


the Banias and Khatris still dominate in zone III (95%), the Jats have come to be more than one third of the commission agents in zone I and II. The scenario of zone III is entirely distinct and still in the traditional mode, where the dominant caste of commission agents is Bania and Khatri and not Jat. The proportion of commission agents belonging to the Bania caste is the highest with 63.75 per cent, followed by Khatri with 31.25 per cent, and Jat being the lowest at 5 per cent. This scenario shows that zone III, popularly known as the cotton belt of the state, still has traditional commission agents like Banias and Khatris. The entry of Jats into this business is still low, which probably may be an indication of comparatively lower crop profitability, low capital formation, caste rigidity, and a trend for non-diversified activities in this zone.

TABLE 2.11: **Caste-wise Distribution of Commission Agents in Punjab (Agroclimatic Zones)**

| *Characteristics* | *Zone I* | | *Zone II* | | *Zone III* | |
|---|---|---|---|---|---|---|
| | *Number of Commission Agents* | % | *Number of Commission Agents* | % | *Number of Commission Agents* | % |
| Bania | 4 | 10.00 | 50 | 27.78 | 51 | 63.75 |
| Jat | 15 | 37.50 | 61 | 33.89 | 4 | 5.00 |
| Khatri | 12 | 30.00 | 38 | 21.11 | 25 | 31.25 |
| Brahmin | 1 | 2.50 | 22 | 12.22 | 0 | 0.00 |
| Rajput | 3 | 7.50 | 4 | 2.22 | 0 | 0.00 |
| Saini | 2 | 5.00 | 1 | 0.56 | 0 | 0.00 |
| Kamboj | 0 | 0.00 | 2 | 1.11 | | 0.00 |
| Others | 3 | 7.50 | 2 | 1.11 | 0 | 0.00 |
| **Total** | **40** | **100.00** | **180** | **100.00** | **80** | **100.00** |

Since caste factor is much more associated with the cultural zones, the caste-wise distribution of commission agents can be better analysed through the Majha, Malwa, and Doaba zones of the state (Table 2.12). Jat commission agents are dominant in Majha, Banias in Malwa, and the Khatri caste is generally dominant amongst commission agents of the Doaba zone of the state. In the Majha zone, Jat commission agents are dominant (67.50%) followed by Bania (12.50%), Brahmin (10%), and Khatri (7.5%) commission agents among the sampled respondents. The proportion of commission agents in the Malwa zone is the highest for Banias (48.89%), followed by Khatris (26.11%), Jats (18.89 %), Brahmins (5.0%), and some other castes namely *Sonar, Ramgharia,* and *Labana*. Similarly, the dominant caste of commission agents in the Doaba zone is Khatri (31.25%), followed by Jat (23.75%), Bania (15.0%), Brahmin (12.50%), and some other castes. The commission agents belonging to the *Rajput* caste are found only in the Doaba zone of the state.

TABLE 2.12: **Caste-wise Distribution of Commission Agents in Punjab**

| *Characteristics* | *Zone I* | | *Zone II* | | *Zone III* | |
|---|---|---|---|---|---|---|
| | *Number of Commission Agents* | *%* | *Number of Commission Agents* | *%* | *Number of Commission Agents* | *%* |
| Bania | 5 | 12.50 | 88 | 48.89 | 12 | 15.00 |
| Jat | 27 | 67.50 | 34 | 18.89 | 19 | 23.75 |
| Khatri | 3 | 7.50 | 47 | 26.11 | 25 | 31.25 |
| Brahmin | 4 | 10.00 | 9 | 5.00 | 10 | 12.50 |
| Rajput | 0 | 0.00 | 0 | 0.00 | 7 | 8.75 |
| Saini | 0 | 0.00 | 1 | 0.56 | 2 | 2.50 |
| Kamboj | 0 | 0.00 | 1 | 0.56 | 1 | 1.25 |
| Others | 1 | 2.50 | 0 | 0.00 | 4 | 5.00 |
| **Total** | **40** | **100.00** | **180** | **100.00** | **80** | **100.00** |

## IV. COMMISSION AGENTS TO FARMERS RATIO

An average commission agent in Punjab state deals with 120 farmers of 71 families and serves farmers from 11 villages (Table 2.13).

TABLE 2.13: **Dealing of the Commission Agents with Farmers in Punjab**

| | |
|---|---|
| Average number of farmers dealing with commission agents | 120 |
| Average number of farm families | 71 |
| Average number of villages served per commission agent | 11 |
| % farm families dealing with the same commission agent for more than one generation | 44.23 |

Changing arhtiyas by the farmers was very rare upto the late 1970s. This phenomenon has started with the entry of non-traditional commission agents in this profession, particularly the Jat arhtiyas. It is interesting to note that about 44 per cent of the farmers are still dealing with the same commission agent for more than one generation. There are so many reasons for this phenomenon. Capitalist development in agriculture has distorted the joint family system and the newly emerged nuclear families have started dealing with the new commission agents. The indebted farmers are not in a position to repay the whole amount of debt in a single season; this, among other factors, is the reason why the farmers remain bonded with the same commission agent. Basically, the change of arhtiya is very difficult as farmers have to take informal clearance from the old commission agents by clearing their dues for joining the new commission agent. Like farmers, the commission agents also have their strong organizations/associations to safeguard the interest of their members. Presently, two commission agent associations are working in Punjab—one is related and associated with the Congress (I) whereas other is politically affiliated with Shiromani Akali Dal (SAD). Both these associations have some norms for commission agents that do not permit practices that can be harmful to other commission agents.

Table 2.14 highlights the zone-wise business deals of the commission agents. It is found that a commission agent in zone I deals with an average 176 farmers from 112 farm families and serves around 26 villages. Similarly in zone III, every commission agent deals with 130 farmers of 74 farm families from 6 villages.

TABLE 2.14: **Dealing of the Commission Agents with Farmers (Zone-wise)**

| *Zone* | *Average number of farmers deal per commission agent* | *Average number of farm families deal per commission agent* | *Villages* | *% of farm families dealing with the same commission agent for more than two generations* |
|---|---|---|---|---|
| Zone I | 176 | 112 | 26 | 36.36 |
| Zone II | 103 | 61 | 13 | 40.38 |
| Zone III | 130 | 74 | 6 | 55.38 |
| Cultural | | | | |
| Majha | 74 | 44 | 9 | 32.43 |
| Malwa | 113 | 66 | 8 | 45.61 |
| Doaba | 159 | 94 | 24 | 45.57 |

However, the number of farm families dealt with by a commission agent in zone II is 61 from 13 villages. This picture shows that the network of commission agents of zone I is widespread over a large number of farmers and in a large number of villages. The cultural zone-wise distribution shows that a commission agent of the Doaba zone deals, on an average, with 159 farmers of 94 farm families from 24 villages. Similarly, in the Malwa and Majha zones, every commission agent deals with 66 and 44 farm families from 8 and 9 villages, respectively.

This shows that in the Doaba zone of Punjab, commission agents have a comparatively vast network in which a large number of farmers from many villages are covered.

## V. FARMERS PREFERENCE

It is a general perception amongst farmers that the behaviour and dealing of the traditional commission agents are good as compared to the non-traditional commission agents. The preferences of the farmers regarding the commission agents of different castes make some of these issues clearer. Table 2.15 and Figure V reveal that about 42 per cent of the sampled farmers preferred to deal with Bania commission agents and 26 per cent opted for those belonging to the Jat caste.

TABLE 2.15: **Farmers' Preference for Dealing with Commission Agents of Different Castes in Punjab**

| *Farmer's Preference* | *Number of Farmers* | *Percentage* |
|---|---|---|
| Bania commission agents | 166 | 41.50 |
| Jat commission agents | 104 | 26.00 |
| Other commission agents | 58 | 14.50 |
| No preference | 72 | 18.00 |

Traditionally, the commission agent system has been largely made of people from the Bania community for whom this occupation is linked to their caste history. However, the surplus of the green revolution has made Jat farmers invest in this occupation, too, as it is more lucrative in terms of returns than agricultural production. This change in the caste composition of the commission agent system seems to be giving rise to new social tensions. The farmers opined that the commission agents from the Bania caste are somewhat polite and humble. Traditionally, they have been hesitant to take over the means of production of the farmers in the case of failure of debt repayment. Nowadays, however, the Jat arhtiyas have no such hesitation. About 15 per cent of the farmers expressed dislike of both Bania and Jat arhtiyas; they

**Figure IV: Farmers Preference for Dealing with Commission Agents of Different Castes in Punjab**

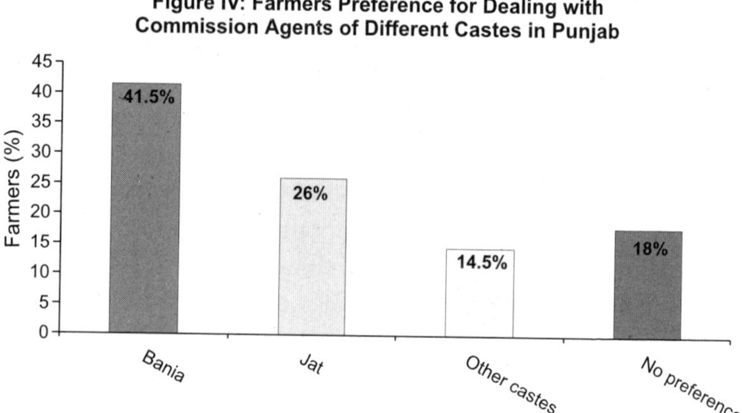


preferred arhtiyas from other castes. It is very interesting to note that 18 per cent of the farmers didn't have caste based preferences. They held that all the commission agents are equally exploitive. And that is a fact because irrespective of their behavioral patterns, the moneylending system itself has become the biggest obstacle for a farmer to ever become completely free from the bondage.

# 3

# Changing Scenario of The Commission Agent System

The terms 'moneylenders' or 'commission agents' (arhtiyas) are synonymous in rural society. A large number of changes have been experienced in this system during British period. However, after independence, a large number of farmers, particularly big farmers, started joining this business. As a result, the scenario of this business has changed considerably. The occupational changes and functional changes along with the new malpractices became the order of the day in this business.

## I. OCCUPATIONAL CHANGES OF COMMISSION AGENTS

Earlier, the commission agent business was an inherited one which was for generations in the hands of particular families from a few castes. With the passage of time, however,, some people from new castes and other professions have joined this business. As a result, the occupational and functional scene of this business has changed. This can be seen from earlier occupations, present occupations, and allied occupations of the commission agents.

### 1. Traditional and Non-traditional Commission Agents

The commission agents are categorized as traditional and non-traditional commission agents on the basis of when they started this business. In the present study, the commission agent families engaged in the business of arhat or commission agent from before the green revolution (mid-1960s), are considered as traditional commission agents. The families, who joined the arhat or commission agent business after the initiation of the green revolution (mid-1960s), are considered as non-traditional commission agents. Table 3.1 reveals that out of a total of 300 sampled commission agents, 23 (7.67%) 'traditional commission agents' were engaged in arhat or commission agent occupation from before the green revolution.

Due to the diversification of the Punjab economy, the proportionate share of traditional commission agents has been declining as new people from other activities of the economy have been joining this business. Thus, the number of non-traditional commission agents has been increasing in the agricultural marketing of the state. In the study survey, the share of non-traditional commission agents came out to be 92.33 per cent.

TABLE 3.1: **Traditional and Non-traditional Commission Agents in Punjab, 2009**

| *Commission agents* | *Number* | *Percentage* |
|---|---|---|
| Total Number of Commission Agents | 300 | 100.00 |
| a) Traditional Commission Agents | 23 | 7.67 |
| b) Non-traditional Commission Agents | 277 | 92.33 |

The zone-wise picture of traditional and non-traditional commission agents is given in Table 3.2.

**Table 3.2: Traditional and Non-traditional Commission Agents in Punjab (Zone-wise)**

| *Zone* | *Traditional* | | *Non-traditional* | |
|---|---|---|---|---|
| | *Number* | *Percentage* | *Number* | *Percentage* |
| **Agroclimatic** | | | | |
| Zone I | 4 | 17.39 | 36 | 13.00 |
| Zone II | 17 | 73.91 | 163 | 58.84 |
| Zone III | 2 | 8.70 | 78 | 28.16 |
| **Cultural** | | | | |
| Majha | 1 | 4.35 | 39 | 14.08 |
| Malwa | 15 | 65.22 | 165 | 59.57 |
| Doaba | 7 | 30.43 | 73 | 26.35 |

The table reveals that in agroclimatic zones, the highest proportion (73.91%) of traditional commission agents falls in zone II, followed by zone I (17.39%), and zone III (8.70%). So far as the cultural zone-wise situation is concerned, Malwa has the highest proportion of traditional commission agents (65.22%) followed by Doaba (30.43%) and Majha (4.35%). This indicates how a large number of new persons have entered the business of a commission agent in zone III and the Majha zone.

*a) Caste-wise Distribution*

The caste-wise distribution of traditional and non-traditional commission agents has been revealed through Table 3.3. It may be observed that during the pre-green revolution period, this business was mainly handled by the *Bania* (60.86%) and *Khatri* (30.43%) castes. This scenario has changed in the post-green revolution period as the *Jat* Sikh caste (28.88%) has emerged as the second leading caste in this profession followed by the *Khatri* (24.55%) and *Brahmin* (7.94%), whereas other castes have a meager share in this profession.

**Table 3.3 Caste-wise Distribution of Traditional and Non-traditional Commission Agents in Punjab**

| *Caste* | *Traditional* | *Non-traditional* | *Total Commission Agents* |
|---|---|---|---|
| **Bania** | 14(60.86) | 91(32.85) | 105 (35.00) |
| **Jat** | Nil | 80(28.88) | 80 (26.6) |
| **Khatri** | 7(30.43) | 68(24.55) | 75 (25.00) |
| **Brahmin** | 1(4.35) | 22(7.94) | 23 (7.67) |
| **Saini** | 1(4.35) | 2(0.72) | 3 (1.00) |
| **Rajput** | Nil | 7(2.53) | 7 (2.33) |
| **Kamboj** | Nil | 2(0.72) | 2(0.66) |
| **Others*** | Nil | 5(1.80) | 5(1.66) |
| **Total** | 23(100.00) | 277(100.00) | 300 (100.00) |

* Others include Sonar, Ramgharia, Labana, and Nai

### *b) Earlier Occupation of Non-traditional Commission Agents*

Our previous analysis revealed that 92.33 per cent of commission agents are new incumbents in this business or have started their business after the green revolution period. Thus, it is interesting to know the earlier occupation of these new entrants. Table 3.4 and Figure VI reveal that out of the total non-traditional commission agents, about 45 per cent came from the farming population, particularly large farmers. With the increase in surplus from the large sized farms, the capital is being invested in this lucrative business to earn more profit through high interest rates and from other businesses. About 24 per cent of the commission agents came from grosser businesses whereas another 31 per cent of commission agents belonged to various types of activities/professions in the economy, such as service, accountants *(muneems)*, traders, financers, and fertilizer/pesticide shop etc.

TABLE 3.4: **Earlier Occupation of the Non-traditional CommissionAgents**

| *Occupation* | *Number of commission agents* | *Percentage* |
|---|---|---|
| Farming | 126 | 45.49 |
| Grosser | 66 | 23.83 |
| Service | 24 | 8.66 |
| Accountant /Muneem | 21 | 7.58 |
| Cloth/Sweet shop owner | 21 | 7.58 |
| Fertilizer/Pesticide shop owner | 7 | 2.53 |
| Factory owner | 2 | 0.72 |
| Cotton trader, Financer & Jeweller | 9 | 3.25 |
| Settled in abroad | 1 | 0.36 |
| **Subtotal** | **277** | **100.00** |

After earning some money from these activities, they further invested this capital in the business of commission agents. Some of these non-traditional commission agents have neither completely shifted to the commission agent business nor are they solely dependent on this business. They have some allied occupations also.

The caste-wise distribution of earlier occupations of commission agents clearly shows that a majority of the Jats came from the farming class. Table 3.5 reveals that out of the total 126 respondents whose earlier occupation was farming, 74 persons belong to the Jat caste.

Similarly, the new entrants into this business came from grocery businesses belonging to the Bania, Khatri, and Brahmin castes. This analysis shows that, although the majority of non-traditional commission agents came from farming and grosser businesses, there were entrants from a variety of other traditional occupations or activities.

TABLE 3.5: **Caste-wise Earlier Occupations of the Non-traditional Commission Agents in Punjab**

| *Occupation/ Caste* | *Total No. of Non-traditional Commission Agents* | *Jat* | *Bania* | *Khatri* | *Brahmin* | *Rajput* | *Kamboj, Saini & Others* |
|---|---|---|---|---|---|---|---|
| Farming | 126(45.49) | 74(92.50) | 11(12.09) | 22(32.35) | 15(68.18) | 3(42.86) | 1(11.11) |
| Grosser | 66 (23.83) | 1(1.25) | 37(40.66) | 23(33.82) | 2(9.09) | 1(14.29) | 2(22.22) |
| Service | 24(8.66) | 3(3.75) | 9(9.89) | 7(10.29) | 1(4.55) | 1(14.29) | 3(33.33) |
| Accountant | 21(7.58) | - | 12(13.19) | 3(4.41) | 2(9.09) | 2(28.57) | 2(22.22) |
| Cloth shop/sweet shop | 21(7.58) | 1(1.25) | 11(12.09) | 9(13.24) | - | - | - |
| Fertilizer/pesticide shop | 7(2.53) | - | 4(4.40) | 2(2.94) | 1(4.55) | - | - |
| Factory | 2(0.72) | - | 1(1.10) | - | 1(4.55) | - | - |
| Cotton trader, Financer & Jeweller | 9(3.25) | - | 6(6.59) | 2(2.94) | - | - | 1(11.11) |
| Abroad | 1(0.36) | 1(1.25) | - | - | - | - | - |
| **Total** | **277(100.0)** | **80(100.0)** | **91(100.0)** | **68(100.0)** | **22(100.0)** | **7(100.0)** | **9(100.0)** |

**Figure V: Earlier Occupations of the Non-traditional Commission Agents, Punjab**

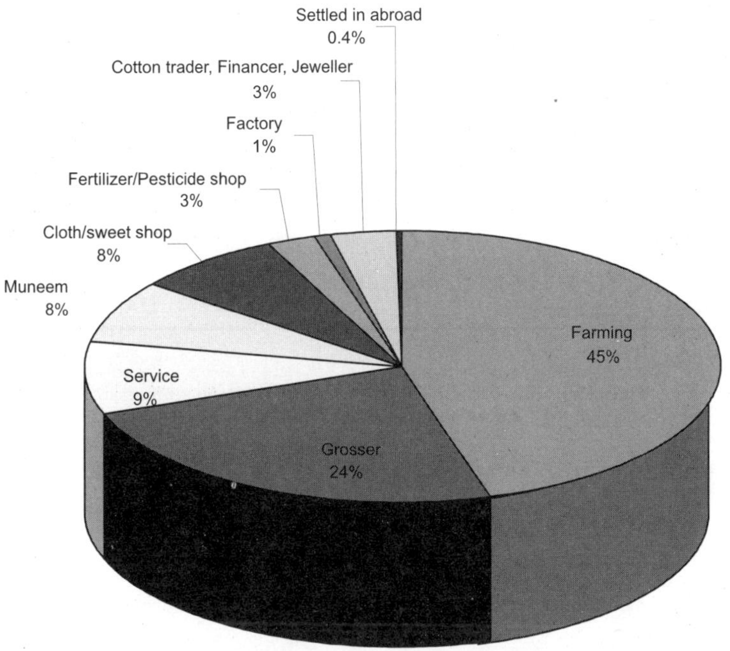


The development of capitalism in the agrarian sector has broken the traditional caste-based activities in the rural economy of the state. Before the green revolution, the Jat community was mainly engaged in farming activities. However, many changes have been experienced after 1970 (Table 3.6; Figure VII). Before the 1970s, there was not even a single Jat family who was engaged in the business of a commission agent in Punjab. It was observed in our field survey that 5 per cent of the the respondent commission agents from Jat families entered into this profession during the 1970s. The process gained momentum after 1980 as 26.25 per cent and 52.50 per cent of Jat families joined this business during the 1980s and 1990s, respectively.

TABLE 3.6: **Trend of Jat Farmers Joining Commission Agent Business, Punjab**

| *Period* | *No. of farmers* | *Percentage* |
|---|---|---|
| Before 1970 | 0 | Nil |
| 1970–1980 | 4 | 5.00 |
| 1980–1990 | 21 | 26.25 |
| 1990–2000 | 42 | 52.50 |
| After 2000 | 13 | 16.25 |
| Total | 80 | 100.00 |

**Figure VI: Trend of Jat Farmers Joining Commission Agent Business in Punjab**

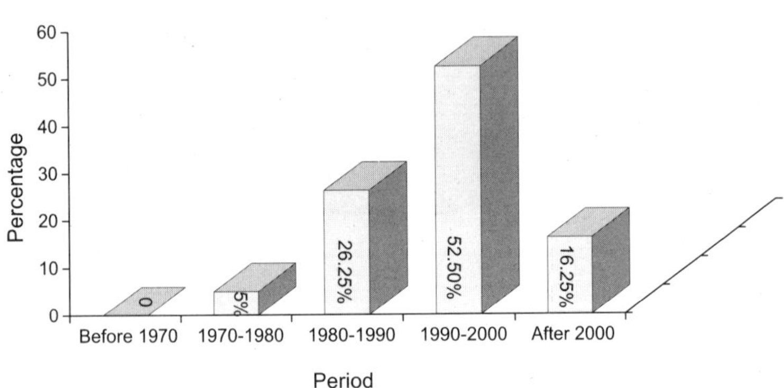


The 1980s and 1990s were the most remunerative phases of the green revolution, as the productivity and market price of crops increased, though at a decreasing rate. The profitability of these crops was maximum during this period. During the 1980s and 1990s, huge agriculture surplus was generated by larger farmers, while on the other hand, reinvestment opportunities within the sector were squeezed. Similarly, the marginal profits from reinvestment in agriculture started declining. This is why the rich peasantry sought to invest in the non-farming sector. Although they invested in rice shellers, transport, farm input shops, commission agent businesses, et cetera. The commission agent businesses, being intimately related to agriculture, emerged a prominent field.

**2. Allied Occupations of Commission Agents**

Commission agents have earned surplus capital from this profession and invested it in other business activities. Some of the commission agents are still involved in only one business; however, a majority of these persons have allied business activities (Table 3.7).

TABLE 3.7 **Total number of Commission Agents Having Allied Occupation in Punjab**

| *Number of Occupations* | *No. of Commission Agents* | *Percentage* |
|---|---|---|
| No other occupation (only arhat) | 125 | 41.67 |
| Commission agent + One allied occupation | 140 | 46.67 |
| Commission agent + Two allied occupations | 31 | 10.33 |
| Commission agent + Three allied occupations | 4 | 1.33 |

It is found that about 42 per cent of the commission agents are dependent only on the arhat business. About 47 per cent of commission agents have one additional business and 10.33 per cent have two additional business activities along with their main occupation. Only 1.33 per cent of commission agents have three additional business activities along with the commission agent business.

In this light, it is very important to view the allied

occupations of the commission agents. Table 3.8 and Figure VIII reveal that as allied businesses, a majority of the commission agents are found doing farming (48%) followed by operating grocery shops (22.29%), owning pesticide/ fertilizer shops (17.71%), rice shelling (16.0%), and other activities such as property dealing, transport, running brick kilns, et cetera (17.14%). All these allied occupations are surviving on the demand created by the peasantry.

TABLE 3.8: **Allied Occupations of Commission Agents in Punjab**

N=175 (Multiple response)

| *Occupation* | *No. of occupations* | *Percentage* |
|---|---|---|
| Farming | 84 | 48.00 |
| Shopkeeper (Grocery+ other shops*) | 39 | 22.29 |
| Pest/fertilizer/seed shop | 31 | 17.71 |
| Rice sheller | 28 | 16.00 |
| Cold store | 2 | 1.14 |
| Other activities** | 30 | 17.14 |

*other shops include cloth merchant, animal feed, bakery, electrician, hardware shop, etc.

**Other activities include cotton mill, property dealer, transport, petrol pump, service, dairy, brick kiln, etc.

The grocery, cloth, pesticide, fertilizer, seed, and animal feed shops are directly related to the rural economy. These are some arhtiyas' own businesses; however, other arhtiyas have associated or linked shops. Commission agents give a slip to the farmers for getting the required domestic articles and farm inputs on credit either from these shops or the connecting shops of their business relatives. They generally charge higher prices and provide commodities of lower quality. This 'slip

**Figure VII: Allied Occupations of Commission Agents in Punjab**

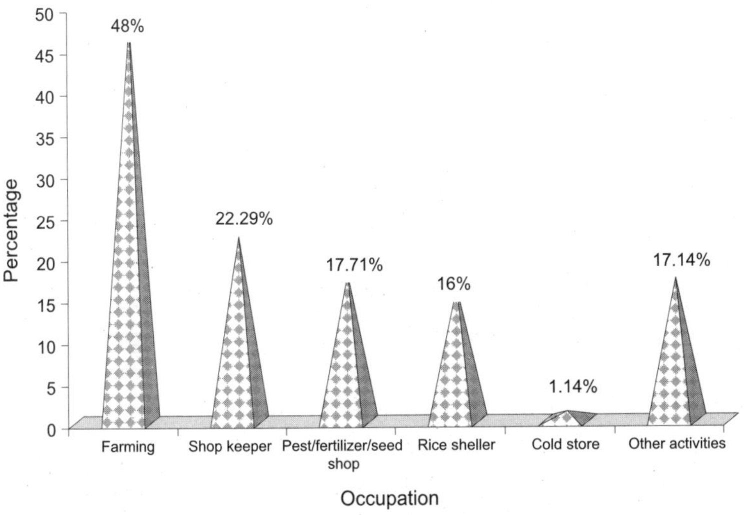


mechanism' always becomes the source of exploitation for these farmers as the debts continue to increase.

This scenario shows that commission agents have invested their money into such types of activities which are related to the farming economy. By and large, the success of these business activities is dependent upon the demand created by the farmers who are dealing with them: farm inputs and domestic articles.

## II. FUNCTIONAL CHANGES OF COMMISSION AGENTS

The change in configuration of the commission agent system, with the entry of new professionals as well as state intervention, has influenced the functioning of this profession over time. The commission agents have changed their modus operandi for enhancing their income or profit margins. They have made a large number of changes in the mode of application and rate of interest on credit advanced and also in the mode and rate of commission on the procurement of farm produce. Moreover, the commission agent system has experienced significant changes in the social relations along with the purchase of land and other means of production of the farmers.

## 1. Change in the Rate of Interest

The rate of interest charged by non-institutional sources, particularly commission agents, has been continuously declining since the mid-1960s. During the 1970s, the rate of interest on non-institutional credit prevailed between the range of 30–40 per cent per annum. The interest rate declined to 24–30 per cent during the 1980s due to the expansion of institutional credit in the agricultural sector. However, in the post-green revolution period, the rate of interest on non-institutional credit further declined to 18–24 per cent per annum during the 1990s. From our field survey, it is revealed that commission agents charge differential rates of interest from different sections of the peasantry. By and large, the rate of interest charged by them declines as the farm size increases. A majority of the small farmers have to pay 24–30 per cent rate of interest whereas the big section of large farmers pay 15–18 per cent of interest on their credit from the commission agents. Commission agents opined that the rate of interest charged from the farmers depends upon their credibility and dealings, irrespective of the size of land holding. Some farmers are very honest and fair in their dealings; so a lower rate of interest is always charged from such types of persons as there is no risk of repayment of credit.

## 2. Deduction of Commission (Arhat) by Commission Agents

The commission agent is the mediator between the sellers and buyers for the marketing of agricultural produce. He facilitates various functions of marketing like the auction of crops and delivery of produce to buyers. He also arranges for the payment to the farmers and labourers for loading/

unloading, cleaning of the produce, along with the required equipment and machines. For performing these functions, the procurement agencies (buyers) pay commission to the commission agents. Presently, this commission is 2.5 per cent of the value of foodgrains marketed in Punjab.

During the early phase of the green revolution (from the mid-1960s to the mid-1970s), the practice of dual arhat was prevalent in agricultural marketing in which the commission was deducted from both the dealing parties (farmers and buyers) by the commission agents. However, during the 1980s, some change took place in deduction of commission practices. The commission agents stopped deducting the commission from the large farmers. However, deduction was continued for the small farmers.

After the 1990s, however, the scenario has totally changed as commission agents stopped charging commission from all categories of farmers. This may have happened due to the awareness and education amongst the farmers. Now, the practice of single arhat is prevalent in which only procurement agencies pay the commission to the commission agents. It is very interesting to note that the large farmers who are not dependent on the commission agents, negotiate with the commission agents for getting some part of commission (arhat) from them.

The market Act envisaged commission from the buyer only. However, the commission agents continued to charge commission from some farmers, to whom they had advanced loans, which generally included the small farmers who were not aware of the illegality of it. As the awareness increased the commission agents stopped charging this commission from the farmers, particularly since 1990. On the other hand, the field survey also reveals that some large farmers negotiate to get 1 per cent to 1.25 per cent of the commission which is paid by the procurement agencies to commission agents. This shows that the large farmers who are educated and have surplus capital are in a position to negotiate everywhere, including with the commission agents. This is the same class that invests money in many allied activities or arhat businesses.

### 3. Change in the Social Relations

An age old myth about 'nail and flesh relationship' (*nauh mass da rishta*) amongst farmers and commission agents is widely publicised in the popular media. The prevalence and relevance of the commission agent system in Punjab's agriculture is claimed by the commission agents on the basis of its existence since generations. Farmers and commission agents have a well-knit relationship as both the parties have blind faith in each other. Nowadays, significant changes have been noticed in this relationship. Our field survey revealed that there is considerable change in the social behaviour of commission agents. Although the traditional commission agents were professionally very smart, they were sober and polite in their dealings. This picture has changed to rudeness and arrogance to some extent due to the entry of Jats into this profession. During the green revolution period, a majority of the commission agents participated in the socioreligious functions of the farmers. Some of the farmers opined that the commission agents definitely attend their functions when they invited them. Moreover, the participation of the commission agents in their functions enhanced their social status. The farmers also participated in the religious functions of the commission agents, in times of sorrow in particular. Large farmers were generally invited by the commission agents to their social functions, particularly on the occasion of their children's marriage. However, the situation has changed as the non-traditional commission agents, particularly Jats, invite all their client farmers irrespective of their holding size.

During the initial phase of the green revolution, food and

shelter was provided to the farmers by the commission agents during the marketing of their crops, as sometimes, farmers had to spend 4–5 days in the market for selling their produce. Nowadays, a large number of villages have the facility of a grain market yard in the village and generally the farmers are able to sell their produce within one or two days. Therefore, the provision of food and shelter is not needed due to the existence of a comparatively efficient marketing system in the state.

**4. Purchase of Farmers' Land**

Punjab is an agriculturally developed but land scarce economy. The ownership of land is an economic asset and has a social prestige in the rural society. The small farmers find it difficult to keep their land intact. The number of operational holdings in the state was 11.17 lakh in 1990–1, which declined to 9.97 lakh in 2000–1. The condition of small farmers (< 5 acres of land) was very precarious as their number had declined from 5 lakh to about 3 lakh during this period. This shows that about 2 lakh small farmers have either leased out or sold off the total or part of their land. A report on the status of farmers who left farming in Punjab states that out of 2 lakh families who left farming, about 36 per cent families have sold their total land whereas another 11.4 per cent of the farming families have sold part of their land (Singh Karam et al, 2007).

The field survey of the study reveals that about 10 per cent of farmers sold their means of production including land, tractor, farm implements, and other assets like livestock, gold ornaments, and trees to repay the loan. Some of these farmers sold their assets even at distress prices due to the continuous pressure of the commission agents.

Another recent field survey on the 'Land Market in Rural Punjab' reveals that in land sales to commission agents by farmers, the buyers were largely non-traditional commission agents (Singh Sukhpal, 2010). This is a new trend of purchasing the land of farmers by commission agents. The traditional commission agents are least interested in purchasing the land of the farmers; if they purchase, they try to recover their disbursed amount by diverting it through the large farmers under some specific mechanism. Sometimes, they extend financial support to medium and large farmers for purchasing the land of indebted farmers. In this way, they recover their loan 'on paper' merely by diverting these loans from distressed peasantry towards medium and large farmers who have a large land base. Unlike the non-traditional commission agents, the traditional commission agents do not buy the land in their own name; instead, they use the name of their linked persons or business relatives.

## III. MALPRACTICES USED BY THE COMMISSION AGENTS

The commission agent uses various modes and strategies for enhancing profitability and successfully developing the business. For achieving this objective, he indulges in all kinds of manipulations of the system. Apart from this, he also indulges in various unprofessional activities and malpractices like non-issuance of J-Forms to the farmers, multiple licensing, practice of damami and the slip mechanism. These practices are not in the interest of either farmers or the government.

### 1. Non-issuance of J-Form

It is mandatory for commission agents to issue J-Forms to the farmers (sellers) for the sale of farm produce. In the J-Form, the details of quantity sold, market charges deducted, and the net payment made to the farmers are mentioned.

Table 3.9 reveals that only about 76 per cent of the selected farmers got this form from the commission agents after the sale of their produce. Even though the issuance of the J-Form is mandatory for commission agents, about 10 per cent of the farmers have been deprived of this right till date. About 14 per cent of the farmers opined that they received this form off and on.

TABLE 3.9: **Farmers' Response for Issuance of J-Form by Commission Agents in Punjab**

| *Farmer's Response* | *No. of farmers* | *Percen-tage* |
|---|---|---|
| Commission agent issues J-Form | 304 | 75.96 |
| Commission agent does not issue J-Form | 38 | 9.62 |
| Commission agent sometimes issues J-Form | 58 | 14.42 |
| **Total** | **400** | **100** |

The non-issuance of the J-Form is beneficial to the commission agents particularly for evasion of taxes, market fee, and for indulging in some other malpractices. This is the main reason why they generally avoid issuing it to the farmers. This practice is harmful to the government and the society including the farmers. The evasion of taxes and market fee is depriving the state of its revenue and possible further investment for development. Due to the non-availability of J-Forms, the farmers also bear losses as they are not able to get the 'bonus price' generally announced late or any other compensation given by the government. The temptation for this malpractice can be well imagined: a one per cent exclusion of produce translates to the commission agent appropriating about 11 per cent of the value of this produce, which is the equivalent of taxes and development funds levied and charged from the buyers who in any case pay these charges. However, this happens only for the private buyers. Similar conclusions are also drawn in another study (Singh Karam, 2009) that generally the commission agents charge entitled commission on the marketing of agricultural produce but in some cases they also attempt to evade putting some quantity sold on record, and thus, in addition to their commission, they also usurp all the other charged amount. In this way, they swell from simple entitled commission of 2.5 per cent to 13.5 per cent of the value of the produce.

### 2. Acquiring Multiple Licenses

Generally, a commission agent would need only one license. Since they resort to malpractices, the licenses can be cancelled. However, this hardly affects the commission agent as he continues to do business on another license in the name of another family member/relative or so. Multiple licensing is another prevalent loophole in the system through which commission agents exploit the state exchequer. Table 3.10 reveals that a large majority of commission agent families have more than one license. An average commission agent in the state has 1.66 licenses.

TABLE 3.10: **Multiple Licensing of Commission Agents in Punjab**

| *Zone* | *Sample size* | *Total number of licenses issued to the sampled commission agent families* | *Average license per commission agents family* |
|---|---|---|---|
| I | 40 | 48 | 1.20 |
| II | 180 | 263 | 1.46 |
| III | 80 | 186 | 2.33 |
| **Total** | 300 | 497 | 1.66 |

The number of licenses with an average commission agent family of zone III is the highest (2.33), followed by zone II

(1.46) and zone I (1.20) licenses. There are many reasons for commission agents possessing multiple licenses. This becomes a means of tax saving as the commission agents divide their expenses and income through many licenses to reduce the income and consequently the sales tax. It is also a means by which penalty is avoided. For example, if the government or Punjab Mandi Board officials cancel their licenses to check such malpractices, commission agents do not have to stop their business and can use another license.

It is a matter of great concern that there is no formality to get this license. If any person has a residential address, he is eligible to get the license for conducting a commission agent business.

**3. Damami**

The amount of commission which the commission agent deducts from the farmer in case of low market arrival, either due to low productivity or crop failure, is called damami. In this practice, the commission agent charges commission from the farmers which is generally equivalent to the previous year's commission. The procurement agencies pay commission to the commission agents as a middlemen. In the case of low marketable surplus, the commission agents receive a lesser amount of commission. In such a case, they deduct money from the farmers' income to fulfill their loss in the commission. Though the practice of damami is an old one, it was not much prevalent during the green revolution period. There was a rising trend of productivity for all the principal crops between the mid-1960s to the late 1980s. This practice came to light in the 1990s when the production of cotton crop reached floor level in 1997 due to a severe attack of the American bollworm. That is why this practice was mainly dominant in the cotton belt (zone III) of the state. In our field survey, about 9 per cent of farmers complained of this deduction. It is a matter of pity that the poor farmer, who gets a poor crop, is further made poorer by the damami of the commission agent.

### 4. Slip Mechanism

Commission agents are not dependent only on the commission agent business, but a majority of them are involved in allied activities. Farmers always demand the money from the commission agents in cash. The commission agent, however, prefers to sell articles to the farmer rather than paying cash. This way the farmer not only remains a bonded seller but also a bonded buyer.

The 'slip mechanism' is being used by the commission agents who issue the 'slip' to the farmers for getting required items from their own shops or connected shops. The price of these articles is always higher than the prevailing market price and they provide comparatively lower quality commodities to the farmers through this slip mechanism. Under this mechanism, the business of commission agents is safe, as they deduct the credit amount from their produce at the time of procurement in the market. Almost all the farmers have mentioned this mechanism during the field survey. This mechanism becomes the source of exploitation of the farmers as well as an efficient business tool for the success of business activities in the market. Even if by this mechanism the commission agent provides quality goods to the farmer at a competitive price, the farmer is bound to lose the 'consumers' sovereignty'.

### 5. Money Advanced and Borrowed by Commission Agents

Farmers get credit from institutional as well as non-institutional sources, especially from the commission agents. An average commission agent advances loans of Rs. 65.74 lakh to farmers. The interest accrued on this amount becomes Rs. 15.78 lakh per annum (Table 3.11). Out of a total debt of Rs. 35,000 crores on Punjab farmers during 2010-11, it is estimated that Rs. 13,300 crores (38%) is advanced by the non-institutional credit agencies in which the commission agent is the major source of finance.

As per law a person involved in moneylending business must register himself as a moneylender. The Punjab Registration of Moneylenders Act 1938 states that the suits for the recovery of loan could be filed by registered moneylenders with a valid license. This law laid an obligation on the moneylender to regularly maintain an account for each debtor separately, of all transactions relating to any loan advanced to that debtor. The government prescribed the manner in which the accounts had to be kept. Moreover, the creditor had to furnish each debtor every six months, with a legible statement of accounts signed by the creditor or his agent of any balance or amount that may be outstanding on 30 June or 31 December.

However, in practice, violations of this Act keep occurring. During our field survey, we experienced that among the respondent commission agents not even a single commission agent was registered for the business of moneylending. To streamline the moneylending system and to provide relief to the farmers, agricultural labour, and rural artisans, the Punjab Relief of Agricultural Indebtedness Bill, 2006 was drafted at the very end of the previous Congress government. Under this Bill, the moneylenders must be registered under the Punjab Registration of Moneylenders Act, 1938. Instead of prevailing very high compounded rate of interest up to 30 per cent, the bill caps at 10 per cent simple interest rate on loans. The formulation of Debt Determination and Settlement Board at every Sub-Division level in the District is a key feature of this Bill, under which the disputed cases up to Rs. 30 lakh of loan can be settled. However, the draft of the Bill was blocked despite approval from the previous cabinet. Even the present SAD-BJP government has submitted in the Punjab and Haryana High Court that the enactment of the draft legislation is 'under consideration'. This matter had come up with respect to public interest litigation on farmers' suicides in Punjab. All the farmers' associations want enactment of this Bill, through which the farmers can get relief from the private moneylenders. However, due to heavy pressure from moneylenders, the Bill has not seen the light of day.

**Table 3.11: Money Advanced and Borrowed by Commission Agents in Punjab**

| *Description* | *Per commission agent* | *Interest on credit/ annum / commission agent* | *@annum* |
|---|---|---|---|
| Advanced money | Rs. 65.74 lakh | Rs. 15.78 lakh | 24% |
| Borrowed money | Rs. 4.03 lakh | Rs. 0.72 lakh | 18% |

Although the fact that farmers always borrow money from commission agents is well known, the source from which commission agents borrow this money is still not documented in any record. In the present study, we tried to get this information but could get little response from the majority of the commission agents. However, some commission agents (9) disclosed that they also borrow money from large farmers, police officials, bureaucrats, and from other servicemen. The rate of interest charged by these people is higher than that of the institutional sources. They disclosed that big farmers who are politically well connected, police officers, and bureaucrats think that their money is always safe with the commission agents from two angles. Firstly, the money can be kept secret as black money and secondly, they can get it back as and when they want through their political power and authority since commission agents will not dare to cheat them.

# 4

# Perceptions Regarding The Commission Agent System

The main purpose of the present commission agent system is to perform the function of being a link between the farmers and buyers by facilitating the marketing and payment of the produce. However, they also engage in the activities of moneylending. There is a debate among academicians, farmer organizations, and commission agents about the role of the commission agent system in the agricultural economy of the state. A large section of academicians and most farmer organizations consider commission agents as merely an exploitative body that has no significant role to play in the procurement of agricultural produce. On the other hand, the association of commission agents and a section of intellectuals emphasised the positive and important role of commission agents in the rural economy. Both these groups logically advance their arguments and opinions. In this light, the views and perceptions of both commission agents and farmers are taken for concluding this debate in a rightful manner.

## I. PERCEPTIONS OF COMMISSION AGENTS

It is a general perception of the common man that the commission agent business is just an easy way of making money. During the survey, only 216 commission agents responded to this query (Table 4.1). There is no denial of the fact that the commission agent business is considered an easy and lucrative venture by the majority (59%) of the commission agents in Punjab. However,, 13 per cent of the respondents considered it a tough and risky job because they always put their money at risk. They always have to keep the cash ready for the farmers but there is no security in the *mandis*. They also lose the interest as the money cannot be deposited in the banks or invested elsewhere. Moreover, they presume that there is always fear of recovery in case of a fall in crop productivity or crop failure altogether, or even in the case of uncertainty like emergencies or mishaps with the farmers.

TABLE 4.1: **Perceptions of the Commission Agents Regarding Commission Agents Business in Punjab (Multiple Response)**

| *Perceptions* | *No. of Commission Agents* | *Percentage* |
|---|---|---|
| Easy and lucrative | 177 | 59.00 |
| Tough and risky | 39 | 13.00 |
| No response | 84 | 28.00 |

The perceptions of the commission agents regarding the commission agent system show a different picture in the different zones of the state (Table 4.2). This business is considered easy and lucrative by majority of the commission agents in zone I (75%) and zone II (65%).

TABLE 4.2: **Perceptions of the Commission Agents Regarding Commission Agents Business in Punjab (Zone-wise Multiple Response)**

| *Perceptions* | *Number of commission Agents* | *%* | *Number of commission Agents* | *%* | *Number of commission Agents* | *%* |
|---|---|---|---|---|---|---|
| **Agroclimatic Response** | **Zone I** | | **Zone II** | | **Zone III** | |
| Easy and lucrative | 30 | 75.00 | 117 | 65.00 | 30 | 16.67 |
| Tough and risky | 0 | 0.00 | 39 | 21.67 | 0 | 0.00 |
| **Cultural Response** | **Majha** | | **Malwa** | | **Doaba** | |
| Easy and lucrative | 14 | 35.00 | 110 | 61.11 | 53 | 66.25 |
| Tough and risky | 1 | 2.50 | 23 | 12.78 | 15 | 18.75 |

However, in zone III about 17 per cent of commission agents admitted that this profession is an easy and lucrative one whereas the majority of them remain silent over this issue. This silence was their answer towards the lucrative nature of this business. It is an established fact that commission agents are very cunning and clever persons. Thus, it is very difficult to get any information from them which is or can be against the interest of these people.

The perceptions of the commission agents regarding sociocultural zones reveal that in the Malwa and Doaba zones about 61 per cent and 66 per cent commission agents, respectively, found this business an easy and lucrative activity. However, in the Majha zone, 35 per cent of commission agents considered it a lucrative business. On the other hand, about 19 per cent of commission agents in the Doaba zone described it as a tough and risky job. Similar views were expressed by 12.78 per cent and 2.50 per cent commission agents in the Malwa and Majha zones, respectively.

## II. FARMERS' PERCEPTIONS

It is an old notion that farmers and commission agents have a closely knit 'nail and flesh' relationship. However, the farmers have never been asked how they perceive this relationship. Thus, in the present study, an effort has been made to highlight the farmers' perception regarding the prevailing commission agent system so that the significance of the commission agent system can be better understood from the angle of the main counterparts.

It is being presumed that the survival of the farmers is not possible without the commission agents. However, the present study breaks this myth and shows that about 84 per cent of the farmers of Punjab State are not in favour of the present system of arhtiyas; they are of the view that the commission agents system should be abolished by the government (Table 4.3). Nevertheless, 16 per cent farmers hold that the present system of commission agents must be kept intact, among them a few farmers confirmed that this system is good enough but there should be some improvements in the system.

TABLE 4.3: **Perceptions of the Farmers Regarding Commission Agent System**

| *Perceptions* | *No. of Farmers* | *Percentage* |
|---|---|---|
| Abolish | 335 | 83.75 |
| Intact | 65 | 16.25 |

For a better understanding of this issue in Punjab agriculture, sampled farmers are further categorized on the basis of socioeconomic characteristics like the size of their land holding, education level, and age of the decision makers in the family (Table 4.4). The chi-square test is carried to test the association of these characteristics with the decision of the farmer whether to keep intact or abolish the prevalent commission agent system in Punjab agriculture. The preferences of the farmers regarding the commission agent system show that nearly 90 per cent of large and semi-medium farmers prefer to abolish the commission agent system. About 31 per cent of the marginal farmers are in support of the existing commission agent system. The value of chi-square is highly significant ($\chi^2$=14.53***) which confers that the decision of the farmers regarding the commission agent system in Punjab is highly associated with the size of the farmers' land holding.

It was assumed that the education level of the farmers is an important variable that might affect the decision of the farmers regarding the role and relevance of the commission agent system in Punjab agriculture. However, our findings reveal that a vast majority of farmers, whether they are illiterate or educated, are not in favour of the present arhtiya system. All the highly educated (postgraduates) farmers also seemed to express views against the commission agent system. It is also interesting to see that even illiterate persons (84.91%) are interested in abolishing the arhtiya system.

The chi-square value came out to be insignificant ($\chi^2 = 4.50^{ns}$), which confers that the education level has no relation to the perceptions of the farmers regarding the commission agent system. Age is considered to be the experience gained; it is always presumed that elderly people make better decisions based on their experiences. In the present study, although about 85 per cent of the farmers above 41 years of age are in support of abolishing the present arhtiya system, the younger ones, too, did not lag behind, more than 80 per cent of whom were also expressive to abolish the system.

TABLE 4.4: **Perceptions of the Farmers Regarding Commission Agent system in Punjab, on the Basis of Socioeconomic Characteristics**

| *Characteristics* | *No. of Farmers* | *Perceptions* | |
|---|---|---|---|
| | | *Intact* | *Abolish* |
| **Size of land holding** | | | |
| Marginal | 45(11.25) | 14(31.11) | 31(68.89) |
| Small | 83(20.75) | 16(19.28) | 67(80.72) |
| Semi-Medium | 135(33.75) | 14(10.37) | 121(89.63) |
| Medium | 60(15.00) | 13(21.67) | 47(78.33) |
| Large | 77(19.25) | 8(10.39) | 69(89.61) |
| | | | $\chi2= 14.53^{***}$ |
| **Education Level** | | | |
| Illiterate | 53(13.25) | 8(15.09) | 45(84.91) |
| Primary | 45(11.25) | 9(20.00) | 36(80.00) |
| Middle | 120(30.00) | 25(20.83) | 95(79.17) |
| Matric | 114(8.50) | 12(10.53) | 102(89.48) |
| 10+2 | 32(8.00) | 5(15.63) | 27(84.38) |
| Graduate | 32(8.00) | 6(18.75) | 26(81.25) |
| Postgraduate | 4(1.00) | 0(0.00) | 4(100.00) |
| | | | $\chi2 = 4.50^{ns}$ |
| **Age Group** | | | |
| ≤ 30 | 36(9) | 7(19.44) | 29(80.56) |
| 31-40 | 127(31.75) | 22(17.32) | 105(82.68) |
| 41-50 | 106(26.50) | 16(15.09) | 90(84.91) |
| >50 | 131(32.75) | 20(15.27) | 111(84.73) |
| Total | 400(100.00) | 65(16.25) | 335(83.75) |
| | | | $\chi2 = 0.57^{ns}$ |
| **Overall** | | | |
| Zone I | 51 | 3(5.88) | 48(94.12) |
| Zone II | 238 | 54(22.69) | 184(77.31) |
| Zone III | 111 | 8(7.21) | 103(92.79) |
| **Total** | **400** | **65(16.25)** | **335(83.75)** |
| | | | $\chi2 = 17.94^{***}$ |

Figures in parenthesis are percentages

Thus, when this was statistically tested, the age of the farmers was not found to be associated ($\chi^2 = 0.57^{ns}$) with the decision in the context of the commission agent system.

The above analysis makes it clear that the decision of farmers regarding commission agent system is closely related to the size of land holding.

## III. PROBLEMS FACED BY THE FARMERS IN DEALING WITH THE COMMISSION AGENTS

A large number of problems are being faced by the farmers in dealing with commission agents in the state as shown in Table 4.5.

TABLE 4.5: **Problems Faced by the Farmers in Dealing with the Commission Agents in Punjab (Multiple response)**

| *Problem* | *Farmers* | |
|---|---|---|
| | *Number* | *%* |
| Recovery of old loan before any payment | 213 | 53.25 |
| Exorbitant rate of interest | 185 | 46.25 |
| Supply of spurious inputs (seed, pesticides etc.) | 158 | 39.50 |
| Malpractices in weighing | 106 | 26.50 |
| High prices for domestic articles | 99 | 24.75 |
| Malpractices in prices | 92 | 23.00 |
| Delay in payment | 76 | 19.00 |
| Practice of damami | 35 | 8.75 |
| Others problems* | 51 | 12.75 |

*Non-issuance of J-Form, signature on blank promissory notes, rude behaviour, kind payment etc.)

Recovery of loan before any payment is the main problem faced by the 53.25 per cent of the respondent farmers. This issue should be seen from both the angles, namely creditors and debtors. It is a general phenomenon that the creditor deducts his loan amount from the debtor, as and when possible. Basically, the logic of the farmer (debtor) guides the situation as there is dire necessity of money for sowing the next crop or fulfilling domestic needs and social obligations. In such a situation, the farmer needs money for farm investment, living expenditure, social festivities, et cetera and other bare necessities of life.

Commission agents charge exorbitant rates of interest on credit which vary from 24 per cent to 36 per cent; this issue is raised by about 46 per cent of the farmers. About 40 per cent of farmers complained that the commission agents supply poor quality seeds and inputs to the farmers. There are many cases in which the farmers faced great loss due to supply of spurious inputs. High prices of domestic articles, malpractices in weighing, and prices of the produce are other major problems pointed out by about 25 per cent of the farmers. Another problem faced by about 19 per cent of farmers is the delay in making the payment for their produce. Damami is such a type of practice in which the commission agent charges the commission from the farmer in case of low market arrivals due to low production or crop failure. The logic of the commission agent for this practice is that they charge low commission from the procurement agencies (buyers) due to low marketable produce. To compensate this loss, they deduct the amount from farmers on the basis of his crop production during previous years. About 9 per cent of the farmers have complained of the problem of damami. Similarly, about 13 per cent of the farmers opined about the rude behaviour of the commission agents, particularly the non-traditional ones. The farmers also complained that commission agents prefer to provide farm inputs and domestic articles on credit basis rather than give them the cash. With the cash money they will be able to buy good quality articles with lower prices. This analysis shows that the farmers have to face a large number of problems in dealing with commission agents in the Punjab State.

# 5

# The Direct Payment System in Agricultural Marketing

Punjab Agricultural Produce Markets (General) Rule, 1962 Sub-Rule 24(II) states that the katcha arhtiya shall make the payment to the seller immediately after the weighing of the produce is over. In the existing marketing system, the payment to the farmers for selling their produce is made through the commission agents. The procurement agencies don't make the payment directly to the farmers; rather they make it through the commission agents. On the other hand, the direct payment norms in agricultural marketing state that the buyer shall make the payment to the seller through account payee cheques. The academicians and farmer organisations are invariably in favour of direct payment to the farmers through cheques. Some of the expert committees have also suggested making direct payment to the farmers through cheques.

Let us take a deeper look into the history of this issue to contextualize the direct payment system in agricultural marketing. In 1961, The Punjab Agricultural Produce Market Act, 1961 was enacted and in 1962, The Punjab Agricultural Produce Market (General) Rules, 1962 were framed. Under these rules, the old rule 11 provides that 'the Katcha arhtiya shall make payment to the seller immediately after the weighment is over.' After this in 1998, the expert committee constituted by Government of Punjab strongly recommended reducing the number of middlemen/intermediaries in the agricultural marketing.The committee suggested that the procurement agencies should directly purchase the farmers' produce at their stores/godowns without the help of commission agents (GoP, 1998). This, however, has still not seen the light of the day. To streamline the marketing system and reduce the dependence on agents in food trade, the committee suggested the following measures:

## EXPERT COMMITTEE RECOMMENDATIONS

1. There should be separate licenses for katcha and pucca arhtiyas under Section 10 of the Act.
2. The bogus licenses or commission agents should be weeded by fixing minimum turnover.
3. The committee recommends that the procurement agencies should directly purchase from their stores/ godowns without the help of commission agents.
4. The state government should declare the silos of the Food Corporation Incorporation (FCI) as purchase centers and the FCI should purchase the wheat in bulk at the silos.
5. Private national or international companies should be encouraged to purchase high quality foodgrain such as wheat (Durum & Triticale) and basmati rice for export direct from the producers bypassing the normal marketing channel and auction system.
6. In order to add value to the farm product and provide alternative channel to the farmers, the processing units, that is, roller flour mills (RFM), oil mills, and fruit and vegetables processing units be allowed to purchase their requirements direct at their premises. To start with RFM (which are 45 in number) should be encouraged for this purpose.
7. '*Apni mandi*' scheme should be strengthened and non-farmers should be encouraged in such farmers' markets.

8. 'Retail markets' where only the producer would sell directly to the retailer, *rehriwalas,* and consumers at a fixed time should be experimented with on the pattern of Hadapsar market near Pune.
9. Separate market yard should be provided and farmers along within the regular fruit and vegetable markets. Farmers with identity card could sell to the retailers and consumers and should be made responsible for giving market fee and RDF to respective market committee.
10. Modern facilities need to be developed especially in the fruit and vegetable markets. Chain of cold stores, cool rooms, washing and grading lines, packing houses, et cetera, should be encouraged by giving subsidies or soft loans to the entrepreneurs in the state.
11. The committee does not favour the private wholesale market at this stage. The processing units would automatically develop into such markets in due course. It is stressed that the Punjab Mandi Board and Market committee should continue to provide better market facilities and infrastructure to reduce the dependence on middlemen in the long-term interest of the farm economy of the state.

The Punjab State Farmers Commission which was constituted in May 2005 recommended the direct payment to the farmer because, being the owner of the agricultural produce, they are entitled to receive payment of the produce from the buyer. The existing system had introduced middlemen called commission agents to receive payment of the farmer produce even though their entitlement is only for a small fee for services rendered by them to the farmers in the market yard. It is a perversity that the owner of the produce has been reduced to the status of a beggar over time. The farmer has to be dependent for his own money from the commission agents who receive hundred percent payment from the buyer as there is no way provided in the rules to ensure a transparent method of payment from the buyer to the seller.

On 31 October 2006, Rule 11 of the Punjab Agricultural Produce Market (General) Rules, 1962 was amended vide which the katcha arhtiya or pucca arhtiya or buyer, as the case may be, shall make payment to the seller through account payee cheques immediately after the weighing is over. If payment is not made, then the same shall be recovered by the market committee concerned, from the katcha arhtiya or pucca arhtiya, or the buyer as the case may be, and shall be made to the seller concerned. This amendment was an outcome of the recommendation of the Punjab State Farmers Commission. However, on 16 November 2006, under the influence of the commission agents association, the Punjab government issued an executive order which stayed the operation of the legislative amendment of the rules.

A group of commission agents led by Balbir Singh Rajewal under the umbrella of Bhartiya Kisan Union (Rajewal) filed a civil writ petition on 31 July 2007 challenging the amendment of the rules that direct payment from the buyer to the seller of the agricultural produce through account payee cheques is against the interests of the farmers. This writ was finally dismissed as infructuous as subsequently the rule was further amended. On 1 August 2008, the writ petition was disposed of on the statement of the counsel for the state of Punjab that they have withdrawn the impugned executive order of 16 November 2006.

The Cotton Corporation of India repeatedly wrote during April and June 2009 to the government of Punjab and Punjab Mandi Board that they do not want to purchase the cotton through commission agents and requested for amendment of the Punjab Agricultural Produce Market Act. Further, the Punjab state agricultural marketing board issued notification on 30 June 2009 that the payment of incidental charges which is to be borne by the seller shall be deducted from the value of the produce to be paid to the seller while making the payment. The payment of the market charges which are to be borne by the buyer shall be paid by the buyer to the market committee. In October 2009, the Punjab government issued the amendment to the Punjab Agricultural Produce Market (general) Rules 1962 and introduced Sub Rule 11 in Rule 24 vide, which again made the commission agent the custodial of the amount that is the right of the farmer as owner of the produce.

The renowned economists S.S. Johl, Sucha Singh Gill, and Karam Singh have described the exploitation and grip of commission agents on the Punjab peasantry. These economists took a strong position against the mode and working of the arhtiya system in Punjab agriculture and stressed for making direct payment to the farmers for the sale of their produce through account payee cheque (Johl 2009,Gill 2009, Singh 2009). This shows that policy makers, farmer organizations, and academicians are in favour of direct payment system in agricultural marketing. On the other hand, a majority of the commission agents do not agree withthis system and are stressing upon the existing system of payment for agricultural produce. They are pressuring the government for keeping the present system of payment intact through their own logic. The current debate also reflects a conflict of interest on this very important issue. For getting an in-depth understanding of this matter, the views of the concerned parties that is, farmers and commission agents, have been taken, so that the issue can be settled.

## I. COMMISSION AGENTS' PERCEPTIONS

The study shows that out of the sampled commission agents only 1.33 per cent are in favour of the direct payment system for crops in Punjab (Table 5.1). These commission agents have their own logic of honesty and faithfulness in the business. All the commission agents of zone III are against the direct payment system of agricultural produce. Similarly, in case of cultural zones, few commission agents (5%) only from the Doaba zone support the direct payment system of crops.

TABLE 5.1: **Perceptions of the Commission Agents Regarding Direct Payment System in Punjab (Zone-wise)**

| *Zone* | *No. of Commission Agents* | *For* | | *Against* | |
|---|---|---|---|---|---|
| | | *No. of Commission Agents* | *%* | *No. of Commission Agents* | *%* |
| **Agroclimatic** | | | | | |
| Zone I | 40 | 3 | 7.50 | 37 | 92.50 |
| Zone II | 180 | 1 | 0.55 | 179 | 99.50 |
| Zone III | 80 | 0 | 0.00 | 80 | 100.00 |
| **Cultural** | | | | | |
| Majha | 40 | 0 | 0.00 | 40 | 100.00 |
| Malwa | 180 | 0 | 0.00 | 180 | 100.00 |
| Doaba | 80 | 4 | 5.00 | 76 | 95.00 |
| **Overall** | 300 | 4 | 1.33 | 296 | 98.67 |

It has been observed that a majority of commission agents opposed the direct payment system of crops; they have given arguments in support of their position (Table 5.2). The major argument against the direct payment is based on the issue of recovery of the loan advanced to the farmers. This problem is highlighted by 79 per cent of the commission agents, followed by the argument of loss of money (33.67%) because the farmers may refuse to repay the loan. It needs to be recalled that they lend the money to the farmers, without being registered as moneylenders and they are worried about recovery for they do not show the money advanced to the farmers on paper records. Another interesting reason given by about 11 per cent of the commission agents is that both commission agent and farmers are dependent on each other. They fear that the implementation of the direct payment system in agricultural marketing will weaken their relationship and both will suffer in the long run. The crop sold by the farmer through the commission agent is the only security as it is the only way to recover the loan advanced to the farmers. This logic is given by 7.33 per cent of commission agents.

TABLE 5.2: **Reasons of Commission Agents for Opposing the Direct Payment System in Punjab (Multiple Response)**

| *Reasons* | *No. of Commission Agents* | *Percentage* |
|---|---|---|
| Recovery problem | 237 | 79.00 |
| Loss of money | 101 | 33.67 |
| Both commission agent and farmer will suffer | 32 | 10.66 |
| Crop is the only security | 22 | 7.33 |
| Negative impact on Punjab agriculture | 11 | 3.67 |
| Extra headache to deal with cheque | 4 | 1.33 |

Finally it is opined by the commission agents that direct payment will have a negative impact on Punjab agriculture (3.67%) because sometimes the farmers demand unplanned loans due to emergency expenditure. In such a situation, the commission agent is the only source of easy and timely help. Moreover, commission agents will have to bear an extra burden to entertain the farmers to get their cheques cleared from the bank (1.33%) because most of the farmers are illiterate and thus hesitant to go through the banking procedure.

The reasons given by commission agents against the direct payment system in agricultural marketing are somewhat different in different agroclimatic and sociocultural zones (Table 5.3).

TABLE 5.3: **Reasons of Commission Agents for Opposing Direct Payment System in Punjab (Zone-wise Multiple Responses)**

| | *Number of Commission Agents* | % | *Number of Commission Agents* | % | *Number of Commission Agents* | % |
|---|---|---|---|---|---|---|
| **Reasons** | **Zone I** | | **Zone II** | | **Zone III** | |
| Recovery problem | 31 | 77.50 | 148 | 82.22 | 58 | 32.22 |
| Loss of money | 16 | 40.00 | 53 | 29.44 | 32 | 17.78 |
| Both commission agent & farmer will suffer | 6 | 15.00 | 14 | 7.78 | 2 | 1.11 |
| Crop is the only security | 7 | 17.50 | 25 | 13.89 | 0 | 0.00 |
| Negative impact on Punjab agriculture | 1 | 2.50 | 10 | 5.56 | 0 | 0.00 |
| Extra headache to deal with cheques | 0 | 0.00 | 4 | 2.22 | 0 | 0.00 |
| | **Majha** | | **Malwa** | | **Doaba** | |
| Recovery problem | 40 | 100.00 | 134 | 74.44 | 63 | 78.75 |
| Loss of money | 0 | 0.00 | 73 | 40.56 | 28 | 35.00 |
| Both commission agent & farmer will suffer | 1 | 2.50 | 12 | 6.67 | 9 | 11.25 |

| | *Number of Commission Agents* | *%* | *Number of Commission Agents* | *%* | *Number of Commission Agents* | *%* |
|---|---|---|---|---|---|---|
| Crop is the only security | 4 | 10.00 | 17 | 9.44 | 11 | 13.75 |
| Negative impact on Punjab agriculture | 2 | 5.00 | 7 | 3.89 | 2 | 2.50 |
| Extra headache to deal with cheque | 0 | 0.00 | 4 | 2.22 | 0 | 0.00 |

In all the agroclimatic zones, recovery problems come out to be the major reason of opposing the direct payment system. It is the highest in zone II (82.22%), followed by zone I (77.50%) and zone III (32.22%). The second major reason for opposing direct payment system is loss of money in all the zones. This reason was given by 40 per cent of commission agents in zone I, about 29 per cent in zone II and about 18 per cent in zone III. Some other reasons like both farmers and commission agents will suffer, crop is the only security and negative impact on Punjab agriculture are outlined by the commission agents of zone I and II.

Similarly, in Majha, all the respondent commission agents feel the risk of recovery of loans. This reason is given by about 79 per cent of commission agents in Doaba and about 74 per cent in Malwa. Loss of recovery was the reason given by the commission agents of Malwa and Doaba zones only. The commission agents of Malwa zone have mentioned the problem of dealing with the cheques as an extra headache for them. In a nutshell, it can be concluded that commission agents are opposing the direct payment system in agricultural marketing mainly due to the recovery system of their loans.

Even after putting the above mentioned reasons and risks, a few commission agents (1.33%) still favour the direct payment system of crops in Punjab (Table 5.4). They opined that there is no risk of recovery of loans because they have an age old relationship with one another. As this business is totally based on faith, the direct payment system will bring more transparency in their dealings, and thus, the farmer would be more satisfied by not having the feeling of being cheated by the commission agent. Some of the commission agents feel that the dignity of their profession has been spoiled by the corrupt commission agents by indulging in malpractices; with direct payment system, their image would be improved and the corrupt ones will leave this profession.

TABLE 5.4: **Reasons of Commission Agents for Favouring the Direct Payment System in Punjab**

| *Reasons* | *No. of Commission Agents* | *Percentage* |
|---|---|---|
| Business based on faith only | 4 | 1.33 |
| More transparency | 4 | 1.33 |
| More satisfaction of the farmers | 3 | 1.00 |

When the commission agents were asked about their reaction regarding the implementation of the direct payment system of crops in Punjab agriculture, they had a mixed response (Table 5.5).

TABLE 5.5: **Reaction of the Commission Agents Regarding the Direct Payment in Punjab**

| *Reaction* | *No. of Commission Agents* | *Percentage* |
|---|---|---|
| Leave the business | 171 | 57.00 |
| Limited/stop advance to the farmers | 112 | 37.33 |
| Protest | 16 | 5.33 |
| No reaction | 1 | 0.33 |

A majority of the commission agents (57%) opined that in such a situation they will leave this profession and would try to opt for the new one. However, about 37 per cent of commission agents may limit or stop the money advances to the farmers. Despite the fact of having a crucial role in the politics of Punjab State, just 5.33 per cent of commission agents have threatened to protest against this decision of the government.

TABLE 5.6: **Reaction of the Commission Agents Regarding the Direct Payment System in Punjab (Zone-wise)**

| | *Number of Commission Agents* | % | *Number of Commission Agents* | % | *Number of Commission Agents* | % |
|---|---|---|---|---|---|---|
| **Reasons** | **Zone I** | | **Zone II** | | **Zone III** | |
| Leave the business | 18 | 57.50 | 99 | 60.56 | 54 | 32.78 |
| Limited/stop advance to the farmers | 14 | 35.00 | 87 | 48.33 | 21 | 11.67 |
| Protest | 3 | 7.50 | 8 | 4.44 | 5 | 2.78 |
| No reaction | 1 | 2.50 | 0 | 0.00 | 0 | 0.00 |
| | **Majha** | | **Malwa** | | **Doaba** | |
| Leave the business | 18 | 45.00 | 126 | 70.00 | 47 | 58.75 |
| Limited/stop advance to the farmers | 28 | 70.00 | 68 | 37.78 | 26 | 32.50 |
| Protest | 0 | 0.00 | 11 | 6.11 | 5 | 6.25 |
| No reaction | 0 | 0.00 | 0 | 0.00 | 1 | 1.25 |

Zone-wise response of the commission agents regarding the direct payment system is depicted in Table 5.6. The argument of leaving the commission agent profession is given by the majority of the commission agents in zone II (60.56%), followed by zone I (57.50%) and zone III (32.78%).

Similarly, the argument of leaving the business is made by 70 per cent of the commission agents in the Malwa, whereas in Doaba and Majha this argument was made by 58.75 per cent and 45 per cent of the commission agents respectively. The commission agents of the Malwa and Doaba zones were in an agitated mood; about 6 per cent opined that they would forcefully protest against the move which breaks the present payment system of agricultural produce in the state.

## II. FARMERS' PERCEPTIONS

The general perceptions of the farmers regarding the direct payment system of crops in Punjab are highlighted in Table 5.7. About 93 per cent of respondent farmers are of the view that the direct payment system will be beneficial for the peasantry of Punjab. In other words, about 7 per cent of the farmers are in favour of the prevailing indirect payment system in agricultural marketing in which the payments are made through commission agents rather than paying directly to the farmers. They remarked that the direct payment of the crops can create problems due to the inefficient banking system of the country.

TABLE 5.7: **Perceptions of the Farmers Regarding the Direct Payment System in Punjab**

| *Perception* | *No. of Farmers* | *Percentage* |
|---|---|---|
| Favoured | 371 | 92.75 |
| Against | 29 | 7.25 |

For a better understanding of these systems in Punjab agriculture, sample farmers are further categorized on the basis of size of land holding, education level, and age of the decision makers in the family. Table 5.8 depicts the views of the marginal, small, semi-medium, medium and large farmers regarding the direct payment in Punjab. It is observed that the direct payment system is highly supported by the large farmers (97.40%) followed by medium (96.67%), semi-medium (92.59%), small (91.57%) and marginal (82.22%).

TABLE 5.8: **Perceptions of the Farmers Regarding the Direct Payment System of Crops in Punjab**

| *Category* | *No. of Farmers* | *For* | *Against* |
|---|---|---|---|
| **Size of land holding** | | | |
| Marginal | 45(11.25) | 37 (82.22) | 8(17.78) |
| Small | 83(20.75) | 76(91.57) | 7(8.43) |
| Semi-Medium | 135(33.75) | 125(92.59) | 10(7.41) |
| Medium | 60(15.00) | 58(96.67) | 2(3.33) |
| Large | 77(19.25) | 75(97.40) | 2(2.60) |
| | | | $\chi2$ = 11.44*** |
| **Education** | | | |
| Illiterate | 53(13.25) | 35(66.04) | 18(33.96) |
| Primary | 45(11.25) | 35(77.78) | 10(22.22) |
| Middle | 120(30.00) | 120(100.00) | 0(0.00) |
| Matric | 114(28.50) | 113(99.20) | 1(0.80) |
| 10+2 | 32(8.00) | 32(100.00) | 0(0.00) |
| Graduation | 32(8.00) | 32(100.00) | 0(0.00) |
| Postgraduation | 4(1.00) | 4(100.00) | 0(0.00) |
| | | | $\chi2$ = 67.66*** |
| **Age** | | | |
| ≤ 30 | 36(9.00) | 35(97.22) | 1(2.78) |
| 31-40 | 127(31.75) | 122(96.06) | 5(3.94) |
| 41-50 | 106(26.5) | 101(95.28) | 5(4.72) |
| >51 | 131(32.75) | 113(86.26) | 18(13.74) |
| **Overall** | **400(100.00)** | **371(92.75)** | **29(7.25)** |
| | | | **$\chi2$ = 12.36*** ** |

Figures in parenthesis are percentages

This shows that as the farm size increases, the proportion of farmers supporting the direct payment system increases. About 18 per cent of the marginal farmers do not want to change the existing system of payment of agricultural produce. On the other hand, just 2.60 per cent of large farmers are against the new system of direct payment of agricultural produce through cheques to the farmers (sellers). The perceptions of the farmers regarding the direct payment system is found highly associated with size of land holding as the value of chi-square ($\chi2=11.44$) is significant at 1 per cent level of probability.

All the educated farmers are in favour of direct payment of crops. It is interesting to note that the majority of illiterate farmers (66.04%) also prefer direct payment of their produce through cheques.

However, about 34 per cent of the illiterate persons are against the direct payment system. Being illiterate, they feel hesitant to deal with cheques. They are of the view that it is a cumbersome process to deal with the banks as there is a lot of paper work, procedural formalities, and bottlenecks in the banks. They find it very difficult to withdraw their money from the banks. The perceptions of the farmers regarding the direct payment system are significantly associated with the level of education of the decision maker as the value of chi-square is 67.66, which is significant at one per cent level of probability. The direct payment system is mainly supported by the farmers below the age group of 50 years. Overall about 93 per cent of the farmers are in favour of the direct payment system. The perceptions of farmers regarding the direct payment system are significantly associated with their age as the value of chi-square ($\chi2=12.36$) is significant at one per cent level of probability. On the whole, it can be concluded that the perceptions of farmers regarding the direct payment system in agricultural marketing are significantly associated with the size of the land, education level and age of the farmers. The larger the farm size, the more the education level and younger the farmer is, and the more in favour of the direct payment through cheque he is.

It is a general perception of the persons who are opposed to the direct payment of agricultural produce that the payment to the farmers for the sale of their produce should not be made through cheques as they are reluctant to go to the banks. For probing this issue, the position of existing bank account of the farmers is examined and the perusal of the results is given in Table 5.9. In Punjab, about 77 per cent of the farmers have their own bank account.

TABLE 5.9: **Farmers Having Bank Accounts in Punjab**

| *Farmer's having bank accounts* | *No. of farmers* |
|---|---|
| Bank account of the respondent | 307(76.75) |
| If not, bank account of other family member(s) | 85(21.25) |
| No bank account of the family | 8(2.0) |

Note: Figures in parentheses are percentages

It is pertinent to note that 98 per cent of families of farmers in the state are dealing with the banks. The Reserve Bank of India has been initiating the scheme of '100 per cent Financial Inclusion' in the country, in which each and every person of the society would come into the banking fold. Under this scheme, there would be a bank account for every person, irrespective of any consideration. So, in the coming period, there would be no person in the society who would not be the customer of the banking system. Thus, the direct payment of the produce through cheques can become successful in the state. This high proportion (98%) of farming community that is already dealing with the banks refutes the logic of arhtiyas for not making payments through cheques, merely on the basis of fear/problems of farmers dealing with the banks.

Table 5.10 highlights the major reasons of the farmers

for favouring and disfavouring the direct payment system in agricultural marketing. The most important reason is to get the full payment of the crops (83.5%) followed by redemption from the clutches of the commission agents (82%), withdrawal of money as per their requirement (72.5%); this also means acquiring the saving habits and more transparency in dealing (70.5%).

Similarly, another reason in support of direct payment system is the availability of better quality farm inputs (69.5%) from independent sources. Otherwise, farmers are supposed to buy inputs from the shops owned by the commission agents. About 61.25 per cent of farmers held that they can repay the loan as per their repaying capacity. Thus, this direct payment system is urgently required for reviving the agrarian economy of the state.

TABLE 5.10: **Reasons of Favouring/Disfavouring Direct Payment System in Punjab**

| *Reasons* | *No. of farmers* | *%* |
|---|---|---|
| **A. Favouring** | **371** | **92.75** |
| Full payment of the crops | 334 | 83.5 |
| Redemption from the clutches of commission agents | 328 | 82.0 |
| Withdrawal of money as per requirement | 290 | 72.5 |
| More transparency | 282 | 70.5 |
| Availability of good quality agricultural inputs | 278 | 69.5 |
| Repayment of the loan according to repaying capacity | 245 | 61.25 |
| Commission agents' easy loan pushes towards more debt | 167 | 41.75 |
| Beneficial for small farmers | 115 | 28.75 |
| Banks will provide more facilities | 93 | 23.25 |

| *Reasons* | *No. of farmers* | *%* |
|---|---|---|
| **B. Disfavouring** | **29** | **7.25** |
| Commission agents lend money at any time on easy terms | 25 | 6.25 |
| Lengthy bank procedure | 20 | 5.0 |
| Farming is not possible without commission agents | 8 | 2.0 |
| Illiteracy | 7 | 1.75 |
| Commission agents & farmers have a strong social relation | 6 | 1.5 |
| Too much time to get the cheque cleared | 5 | 1.25 |
| Commission agents never cheat honest farmers | 5 | 1.25 |
| Banks will not wait for recovery | 4 | 1.0 |
| How the small farmer will survive | 4 | 1.0 |
| Purchasing agencies will start exploiting the farmers | 3 | 0.75 |
| Nobody will take the responsibility of sale of produce | 2 | 0.5 |
| Farmer will not be able to manage the full payment | 1 | 0.25 |

It has also been observed (Table 5.10) that even after having many points in favour of the direct payment, it has been opposed by only about 7 per cent of the farmers of whom about 6 per cent of the farmers opined that they will not be able to get money at any point of time whereas in the prevailing commission agent system they can get it at any time on easy terms. 5 per cent of the farmers complained that the banking procedure is so lengthy and cumbersome that they would not be able to get the money. About 2 per cent of the farmers offered the logic that due to illiteracy they would have to depend on others to deal with banks.

Similarly, just 1 per cent of the farmers complained that it would take too much time to get the cheque cleared, hat the small farmers could survive without commission agents, that nobody would take the responsibility of the sale of produce, and that the commission agents would never cheat honest farmers were some of the reasons given by a small section of the farmers who were against the direct payment system in agricultural marketing of the state.

All these reasons mentioned by the farmers against direct payment system raise a question mark on the efficiency of the banking system of the state. Basically, these views are expressed by the farmers in the context of prevailing conditions and functioning of the banking system. An efficient and farmer-friendly banking system may not only be the sound substitute for the commission agent system but also be an effective agent for solving all their problems related with financial market.

# 6

# Increasing Indebtedness; Increasing Dependency

It is now a well known fact that the Punjab peasantry has been living under severe debt. The green revolution model increased the financial need of the farmers, further increasing their dependency on non-institutional sources of finance. Not only non-institutional sources but institutional sources of finance have exploited the farmers through heavy interest rates and high transaction costs of their loans.

The productivity of almost all the crops is high, but the profitability is quite low in Punjab. Thus, the peasantry is reeling under debt. On an average, about 90 per cent of the farmers of the state are under debt (Table 6.1). The position of medium and semi-medium farmers is very precarious as about 95 per cent and 98 per cent farmers of these categories, respectively are indebted. The capitalist model of agriculture has made almost all the categories of farmers indebted. Not only small farmers but about three-fourths of the large farmers who have land holding of more than 6 hectares are also living under debt. The lack of agricultural growth, meanwhile, is evident from figures. Agricultural growth in Punjab State was 4.6 per cent in the 1980's which declined to 2.5 per cent in the 1990s. Unfortunately, it was even lower than the national average growth rate of 3.2 per cent in the 1990s. The growth rate of Punjab agriculture further decelerated to 1.9 per cent in the 2000s. This distinct slowdown in agricultural growth has adversely impacted the socioeconomic base of the rural community. There seems to be little doubt left to the mind as who is profiteering from the indebtedness. From banks and big farmers to arhtiyas and other petty moneylenders, moneylending seems to be the most lucrative business.

TABLE 6.1: **Extent of Indebted Farm Households in Punjab, 2008–9**

| *Size of holding* | *Average Farm Size (ha)* | *Sample Size* | *No. of Indebted Households* | *Percentage of Indebted House holding* |
|---|---|---|---|---|
| Marginal | 0.75 | 45 | 39 | 86.67 |
| Small | 1.63 | 83 | 73 | 87.95 |
| Semi-Medium | 2.96 | 135 | 128 | 94.81 |
| Medium | 5.10 | 60 | 59 | 98.33 |
| Large | 7.85 | 77 | 61 | 79.22 |
| Average | 3.73 | 400 | 360 | 90.00 |

Despite the fact that institutional network of finance has been significantly developed in the state, the non-institutional sources, particularly commission agents are still the important source of credit to the Punjab farmers. Table 6.2 reveals that about 36 per cent of the total credit of Punjab farmers is being advanced by the commission agents. This proportion is slightly higher in case of smaller farmers than the larger farmers as the larger farmers have a better access to institutional loans.

TABLE 6.2: **Magnitude of Farmer's Debt in Punjab, 2008–9**

| *Size of* | *Debt/ House hold* | *Debt/ha* | *Institu- tional* | *Non-institutional Commission agents* | *Others** |
|---|---|---|---|---|---|
| Marginal | 119548 | 159397 | 71012 (59.4) | 46385 (38.8) | 2152 (1.80) |
| Small | 186652 | 114510 | 112178 (60.1) | 70741 (37.9) | 3733 (2.0) |
| Semi-Medium | 348638 | 117783 | 213367 (61.2) | 127950 (36.7) | 7321 (2.10) |
| Medium | 357381 | 70074 | 227295 (63.6) | 122224 (34.2) | 7862 (2.20) |
| Large | 514515 | 65543 | 341638 (66.4) | 160940 (31.28) | 11937 (2.32) |
| Average | 322496 | 86460 | 199948 (62.00) | 116099 (36.00) | 6450 (2.00) |

* *Others include shopkeepers, relatives, and friends*

The Punjab farmers are indebted to the tune of Rs. 322,496 per sample household. The amount of debt is directly related to farm size. It is the highest in case of large farmers and the lowest in case of marginal farmers. However, in relation to the size of land, the association is negative. The per hectare debt is Rs. 159,397 on marginal farmers and Rs. 65,543 on large farmers. This shows that the relative indebtedness on the smaller farmers is about two times that of the larger farmers.

TABLE 6.3: **Increasing Debt Burden on Punjab Peasantry—Various Estimates**

| *Year* | *Institutional (Rs./crore)* | *Non-Instional (Rs./crore)* | | *Total Debt (Rs./crore)* | *Studies* |
|---|---|---|---|---|---|
| | | *Commission Agent* | *Others* | | |
| 1997 | 2654 (46.56) | 2641 (46.32) | 406 (7.12) | 5700.91 (100.00) | Shergill (1998) |
| 2002–3 | 4139 (41.87) | 4994 (50.51) | 753 (7.62) | 9886 (100.00) | Singh & Toor (2003) |
| 2005–6 | 13047 (61.94) | 6736 (31.98) | 1281 (6.08) | 21064) (100.00) | Singh, Kaur & Kingra (2007) |
| 2007–8 | 15407 (50.69) | 13179 (43.36) | 1808 (5.95) | 30394 (100.00) | Shergill (2010) |
| 2009–10 | 19995 (62.00) | 11610 (36.00) | 645 (2.00) | 32250 (100.00) | Present study |

The declining phase of the green revolution started in the early nineties as the farm profitability was the lowest in mid-1990s. During this period, economists, popular discourse, and media started raising a hue and cry regarding the worst economic position of peasantry. In this critical period, the first popular report brought out by H.S. Shergill (1998), which was widely circulated among scholar, media, and policy planners. The report highlighted that Punjab peasantry was indebted of Rs. 5,700 crores in 1997, out of which 46.32 per cent was owed by the commission agents. After five years, another study concluded by Singh and Toor (2003) showed that the debt burden on Punjab peasantry increased to the tune of Rs. 9,886 crores, out of which the share of commission agents was 50.51 per cent. In 2005–6, Singh, Kaur, and Kingra (2007) estimated that the debt burden on Punjab farmers has increased to Rs. 21,064. The share of commission agents, though, increased in absolute term, but significantly declined from 51 per cent to 31.98 per cent due to liberal credit policies of the government for agricultural sector. Recently, H.S. Shergill (2010) again conducted study on farmers' debt and estimated that the debt burden on Punjab farmers increased to Rs. 30,394 crores. The share of the commission agent was 43.36 per cent in 2007–8. Similarly, our present field survey revealed that the Punjab farmers are indebted to the amount of Rs. 32,250 crores during 2009–10. The share of the non-institutional source is 38 per cent out of which Rs. 11,610 crores (36 per cent of total debt) owed by the commission agents (Table 6.3). This scenario shows that the debt burden on Punjab peasantry has been significantly increasing since the mid-1990s. This phenomenon is said to be the phase of falling farm profitability and increasing indebtedness. The analysis also conferred that the commission agents have still dominant status in rural lending market

TABLE 6.4: **Magnitude of Institutional Loans to Punjab Agriculture (Rs. Crores)**

| *Year* | *Commercial Banks* | *Primary Agricultural Cooperative Societies* | *State Agricultural Development Banks* | *Total* | *NSDP from Agriculture and Livestock* | *Total Institutional Debt as per cent of NSDP* |
|---|---|---|---|---|---|---|
| **1970–1** | 20* | 52 | 48 | 120 | 830 | 14.46 |
| **1980–1** | 235 | 146 | 109 | 490 | 2156 | 22.73 |
| **1990–1** | 1070 | 482 | 311 | 1863 | 7393 | 25.20 |
| **1995–6** | 1655 | 756 | 551 | 2962 | 15374 | 19.27 |
| **2000–1** | 3120 | 1530 | 1556 | 6206 | 25596 | 24.25 |
| **2001–2** | 3476 | 1740 | 1663 | 6879 | 26440 | 26.02 |
| **2002–3** | 4425 | 2084 | 1679 | 8188 | 25554 | 32.04 |
| **2003–4** | 5567 | 2319 | 1769 | 9655 | 27853 | 34.66 |

| *Year* | *Commercial Banks* | *Primary Agricultural Cooperative Societies* | *State Agricultural Development Banks* | *Total* | *NSDP from Agriculture and Livestock* | *Total Institutional Debt as per cent of NSDP* |
|---|---|---|---|---|---|---|
| **2004–5** | 6644 | 2665 | 2012 | 11321 | 29152 | 38.83 |
| **2005–6** | 8149 | 3035 | 2113 | 13297 | 31664 | 41.99 |
| **2006–7** | 9863 | 4115 | 2175 | 16153 | 35873 | 45.03 |
| **2007–8** | 12094 | 4115 | 2059 | 18268 | 43451 | 42.04 |

Note: *Derived from the 1975 figure of direct advances of Rs. 27 crores (Karam Singh, 2009)

Source: Government of Punjab, Statistical Abstract of Punjab, various issues.

Since the initiation of the green revolution in the mid-1960s, the money financed to agricultural sector by institutional sources has increased over time. The direct finance to farmers by the commercial banks, Punjab Agricultural Cooperative Societies and State Agricultural Development Banks increased significantly. Total credit advanced by the commercial banks increased from Rs. 20 crores in 1970–1 to Rs. 235 crores in 1980–1, Rs. 1070 crores in 1990–1 and further 12,094 crores in 2007–8 (Table 6.4). The cooperative sector has played an important role for advancing credit to the farmers of the state. The credit advanced by the Punjab Agricultural Cooperative Societies and State Agricultural Development Banks was Rs. 100 crores during 1970–1 which increased to Rs. 255 crores in 1980–1, Rs. 793 crores 1990–1 and Rs. 6,174 crores in 2008–9. The Punjab Agricultural Cooperative Societies have been providing short-term loans to farmers for agricultural inputs. Basically, these societies have been providing agricultural inputs especially fertilizer to the farmers at their door steps. As these societies have direct relations with the farmers, their repayment or recovery performance is fairly good. Despite the fact that these societies/banks make some book adjustments for the recovery of their loans, yet their repayment performance was fairly good till the end of the 1990s. After this, the agrarian crisis surfaced. As the productivity reached its lowest ebb and profitability declined to the floor level, the peasantry was engulfed in a severe debt trap. Thus, recovery of cooperative credit and other institutional and non-institutional credit could not be made by the Punjab peasantry.

The Net State Domestic product (NSDP) from agriculture and livestock increased from Rs. 830 crores in 1970–1 to Rs. 2,156 crores in 1980–1, Rs. 7,393 crores in 1990–1 and further Rs. 43,451 crores in 2007–8. Similarly, the total institutional debt as proportion to NSDP also increased from 14.46 per cent in 1970–1 to 22.73 per cent in 1980–1 and further 25.20 per cent in 1990–1. It slightly declined to 19.27 per cent in 1995–6 and further start increasing to 24.25 per cent in 2000–1 and presently 42.04 per cent in 2007–8. This shows that magnitude and proportionate share of institutional debt has been increasing in Punjab agriculture.

No doubt, the institutional agricultural credit has increased over time in Punjab State, but still this amount was not adequate enough which could fulfill all the requirements of the farmers. Moreover, the cumbersome and time consuming credit delivery system pushed the farmers towards private money lenders.

It is a well known fact that institutional source of finance has vast access to the rural landing market as there are more than 1000 bank branches of Scheduled Commercial Banks, 89 State Agricultural Development Bank (SADB) branches and 3990 Primary Agricultural Cooperatives Societies (PACS) in the state. The total membership of PACS and SADB is about 30 lakh and the farmers membership of commercial banks is about 7 lakh. Our field study also conferred that about 98 per cent farmer families have their accounts in the banks. This means that out of a total 10 lakh farm families of the Punjab State, about 9.80 lakh families have already been dealing with the banks.

TABLE 6.5: **Linkages Between Money Advanced and Farm Produce Sold Through Commission Agents, Punjab (Rs. per household)**

| *Size of* | *Farm produce sold through Commi-ssion agent* | *Credit advanced by Commi-ssion agents* | *Gap between credit and value of crop* |
|---|---|---|---|
| Marginal | 47831 | 46385 | 1446 |
| Small | 111586 | 70741 | 40845 |
| Semi-Medium | 225379 | 127950 | 97429 |
| Medium | 397528 | 122224 | 275304 |
| Large | 663668 | 160940 | 502728 |
| Overall | 283172 | 116099 | 167073 |

Although the main function of the commission agent is to act as a middleman between the procurement agencies and the farmers for the marketing of the produce, this function seems a secondary one as the commission agent is involved mainly in the transaction of money to the farmers. The whole produce of the farmers is being procured through the commission agents. The procurement agencies make the payment of the farmers to the commission agent and then the commission agent pays the same amount to the farmers after deducting all types of dues.

Out of the total credit advanced to the farmers, about 36 per cent is solely supplied by the commission agent. From this fact, it seems the commission agents are performing a very good job in the agricultural economy of the state as they are advancing big amounts of loan to the farmers without any security. This aspect can be seen from the perspective of ground reality. Actually, the farmers of the state sell their produce through the commission agents, which becomes the security or guarantee of the loan advanced to the farmers by the commission agent. The Punjab farmers on an average sell produce worth Rs. 283,172 through the commission agents (Table 6.5). Obviously, this amount of produce is different for various farm categories and increases with the size of land ownership. The value of farm produce sold through the commission agent is Rs. 47,831, Rs. 111,586, Rs. 225,379, Rs. 397,528 and Rs. 663,668 on marginal, small, semi-medium, medium and large farmers, respectively. On the other hand, the credit advanced to these farmers by the commission agents is lower on all the farm categories. In this way, after repayment of the loan of the commission agent, the farmers save some amount for the repayment of the institutional loan as well as fulfillment of domestic and social needs. The amount of such saving is Rs. 167,073 with an average farmer of the state, which increases with the size of farm. This amount is Rs.1446, Rs. 40,845, Rs. 97,429, Rs. 275,304 and Rs. 502,728 for marginal, small, semi-medium, medium, and large farmers, respectively. This analysis shows that commission agents advance loans to the farmers on the basis of their value of produce. As the farmer is almost compelled to sell his produce through the commission agent, so is the repayment of all type of credit/loans thus assured to the commission agent. This reveals that there is a direct link between the marketable surplus of farmers and amount of credit advanced by the commission agents to the farmers.

The non-institutional source of finance pushes the farmer under severe debt burden. On the one hand, rate of interest charged by non-institutional sources, is significantly higher than that of institutional sources. Generally the rate of interest is always high in those situations where repayment of credit is poor and uncertain. However, in the present situation, the repayment of loan is assured as the farmer is bound to sell his produce through the commission agent. The procurement agencies release all the payment of the produce to the commission agents and then the commission agents after deducting all their dues, make the payment to the farmers. Under such a situation when the repayment is so assured, then at least the rate of interest of commission agents should not be higher than that of the institutional sources.

Another aspect is related to the debt waive-off issue of the farmer by the government. Due to high proportion of non-institutional debt amount, the farmers of the Punjab could not get benefit of the debt waiver scheme of union government in 2008. Although the Punjab farmers are highly indebted as the magnitude of debt is high among all the states of Indian Union. Out of the total debt waiver amount of Rs. 65,000 crores, Punjab could get Rs 1,200 crores (1.85 %). This meager amount is merely an eye wash as it serves only 3 per cent of the total debt burden on Punjab peasantry. Sometimes, it is said that Punjab farmers are well-to-do and their loan repayment is high; that is why they could reap least benefit of debt-waiver scheme. This argument is far from reality. Due to the high proportion of non-institutional debt, the Punjab framers were deprived of the benefit of the debt-waiver scheme. In this way, the non-institutional loan of the farmers has played a key role in making and keeping the farmer under debt.

## FARMERS' SUICIDES

Farmers are under debt. Moreover, they are under non-institutional debt. Private moneylenders not only charge exorbitant rates of interest but engage in a large number of unethical practices for the maximum possible exploitation of the peasantry. For the debt servicing of private moneylenders, they start selling all their valuable assets like ornaments, trees, and animals. The family comes under depression and severe economic distress when they sell their means of production, especially land and tractor. In some situations where the debt burden pushes the farmers into unbearable stress levels, they prefer to finish their lives. The pressure or insult by the moneylenders work as a catalyst to force the farmers toward the act of committing suicide.

Suicide is a complex interplay of multiple causes that are not mutually exclusive. During last one decade several studies were conducted by the scholars (Table 6.6). All the studies conferred similar conclusions that farmers and agricultural labourers have been committing suicides primarily due to economic hardship and indebtedness. Small and marginal farmers are the main victims, as they are not in a position to eek out their lives with meager earnings reaped from their tiny size of holdings, which, of course, are capital intensive. The large numbers of suicide victims were indebted either exclusively to private money lenders or both the private and public agencies.

TABLE 6.6: **Suicides in Rural Punjab—Various Studies**

| *Item* | *Bhalla et al. 1998* | *Iyer and Manic 2000* | *AFDR 2000* | *Chahal 2005* | *PAU 2009* |
|---|---|---|---|---|---|
| Suicide cases studied (No.) | 53 | 75 | 79 | 42 | 2890 Census |
| Cultivator(%) | 55 | 67 | 85 | 100 | 60 |
| Agricultural labour(%) | 45 | 33 | 15 | - | 40 |
| Small and marginal farmers(%) | 25 | 84 | 66 | 55 | 79 |
| Suicides due to debt (%) | 38 | 79 | 62 | 55 | 73 |
| Debt exclusively | 37 | 68 | 27 | 9 | N.A. |

| *Item* | *Bhalla et al. 1998* | *Iyer and Manic 2000* | *AFDR 2000* | *Chahal 2005* | *PAU 2009* |
|---|---|---|---|---|---|
| from money lenders (%) | | | | | |
| Debt from money lenders and others (%) | NA | 81 | 74 | 52 | 90 |

Sources: Bhalla et al. (1998), Iyer and Manick (2000), AFDR (2000), Chahal (2005) and PAU (2009)

The first ever census survey on the issue of farmers and agricultural labourers suicides was conducted by Punjab Agricultural University, Ludhiana (PAU, 2009). The study revealed that as much as 2,890 farmers and agricultural labourers have committed suicide in the Bathinda and Sangrur districts during 2000–8. Although National Crime Record Bureau (NCRB) data focuses the Punjab state among the least suicide prone areas of the country but PAU census survey revealed that the number of farmers' suicides is far higher than that of the figure provided by the NCRB.

Moreover, the farmers' suicide rate is almost one-and-half times more than the general suicide rate. According to NCRB data, almost 15 farmers per lakh farmers annually had committed suicide in India since 1997. This figure for general suicide is just 10. The PAU census survey conferred that the farmers' suicide rate is four times more than that of the figure provided by the NCRB (63 against 15). It is also important to know that 79 per cent of these farmers are the owners of less than 2 hectares of land and about 73 per cent were under the stress of heavy debt burden of commission agents and banks.

Although the tone and tenor of the state and the popular discourse have been raising sociological and psychological aspects as the primary reasons for this suicide phenomenon, the suicide phenomenon is purely an economic one. However, in some situations, this economic aspect is triggering them towards the other non-economic factors. Declining farm profitability in general and debt burden from private money lenders in particular, are the main reasons behind this act of finishing precious human lives.

# 7

# Conclusions and Recommendations

The commission agent, popularly known as arhtiya, is the most dominant person in the agricultural marketing system of the state. Traditionally, arhtiyas have emerged from petty shopkeepers and merchants who provide domestic consumable articles on credit and are also involved in the activity of moneylending. It was trading in agricultural produce which brought them close to peasants and the wholesale traders. The dominant problem of indebtedness in Punjab agriculture was highlighted by M.L. Darling in the 1920s, when it was reported that nearly four-fifths of the Punjab peasantry was under debt. At that time, the proportionate share of moneylenders in the total population in Punjab was five times more than in the rest of the country.

The green revolution of Punjab made the agricultural production process of the state highly mechanized, capital intensive, and commercialized. Though Punjab agriculture had achieved high growth for a long time up to the early 1990s, it slowed down thereafter, leading to increasing costs, shrinking resource base, declining productivity, falling profitability, and mounting indebtedness. The role of commission agents has further aggravated the problems of the peasantry and thus the process of marginalisation and de-peasantisation has started in the Punjab state.

Keeping in view the above said agrarian crisis and the role of commission agents, the present study has been conducted to examine the status of the commission agent system in Punjab. The relevance of payment for crops to the farmers, through middlemen or cheques, is an important issue for understanding the market imperfections in the state's agriculture. Thus, this study has focused on examining the role and status of the commission agent system with special reference to the direct payment system in the agriculture sector. The study is mainly based on the primary data collected from commission agents and farmers which relate to the agricultural year 2008–9.

The primary data regarding commission agents were collected from 15 grain markets. A sample of 40 commission agents from the sub-mountainous zone, 180 from the central zone, and 80 from the south-western zone was selected, choosing 20 commission agents from each market. Thus, a total of 300 commission agents were selected for the study. Similarly, a sample of 400 farmers was taken from the adjoining villages of the selected markets. In this way, a total sample of 700 respondents, comprising 300 commission agents and 400 farmers was taken for the study.

In Punjab agriculture, commission agents perform the function of becoming a link between the farmers (sellers) and buyers (consumers, wholesalers, procurement agencies, et cetera) for facilitating the auction and delivery of the produce to the buyers. They arrange for the payment to the farmers (sellers) and other facilities like loading/unloading and cleaning of the produce. They also make arrangements for the required equipment and machines for weighing, filling, and stitching grain bags, though the farmers and buyers pay for these services. They also provide agricultural inputs, domestic articles, and money to the farmers. The relationship between commission agents and farmers has remained a vexed one. It has been reported since a considerable length of time that farmers are being increasingly exploited through all these transactions, especially with the worsening of the agrarian crisis. Commission agents exploit the farmers by charging an exorbitant rate of interest, supplying spurious farm inputs, and through other various malpractices in marketing activities. Due to the exploitative network of commission agents, some academicians and policy makers had strongly suggested reducing the role of market intermediaries or to regulate the commission agent system in the agricultural sector.

Although the Punjab Mandi Board issued a total number of 33,975 licenses of katcha arhtiyas (commission agent) for grain marketing of the state, the actual number of commission agent families working in the grain markets is 20,232. The number of commission agent families is the highest (13,752) in zone II, followed by zone III (5,416) and zone I (1,064).

Commission agents had a long history in the agrarian economy of the state. Before the green revolution, their role was limited to moneylending but during the post-green revolution period, their mode of functioning and status has changed significantly. Being the middlemen in agricultural marketing, commission agents charge commission from the buyers. The rate of commission was fixed at the rate of 1.50 per cent off the value of farm produce as of 26 May 1961 on ad valurem basis. However, being a strong lobby, commission agents could manage an increase in commission from time to time with their continuous pressure on the state government. The rate of commission was raised to 2.00 per cent on 11 April 1990 on all the agricultural commodities. On 22 May 1998, the commission was again raised to 2.50 per cent on all these crops. It is estimated that commission agents have earned about Rs. 6,427.47 crores from 1989–90 to 2009–10 on the marketing of all the commodities in the state. On an average, the commission agents earned commission amounting to Rs. 306.07 crores per annum since 1989–90. Despite the fact that commission agents do not have any significant role in the procurement of those crops (wheat and paddy) in which assured marketing prevails, they are able to increase their commission from time to time. This could happen due to the continuous pressure of this lobby, otherwise there is no point inincreasing their commission, which was and remains fixed on ad valurem basis. As the value of produce increases over a period of time and the market arrivals and prices increase every year, the arhtiyas' commission automatically increases.

It is observed that the majority of the commission agents (59%) fall in the age group of 31 to 50 years and only 7.33 per cent are found below 30 years. To get deeper information about the social characteristics of the commission agents, it has been observed that the proportion of the younger (dH30 years of age) commission agents is higher (10%) in zone III whereas the proportion of persons between the ages of 31 to 40 years is higher in zone II. The proportion of the younger commission agents is high in the Malwa zone whereas the proportion of middle aged (41–50 years) commission agents is high in the Majha zone.

Education level indicates that 37 per cent of commission agents are graduates and only 7 per cent are below matric level of education. It is very interesting to note that 1.67 per cent of the commission agents do not have any formal education whereas, 2.33 per cent of commission agents are postgraduates. This shows that the persons with different levels of education have been working in this business.

The education level of commission agents also differs in different agroclimatic zones. In zone I, no illiterate or postgraduate person could be found in this business. On the other hand, the proportion of commission agents who do not have any formal qualification is 1.67 in zone II and 2.50 in zone III. There are some commission agents in these zones who are well educated, even up to the postgraduation level. Similarly, the education level of commission agents in different cultural zones of the state is also different. No illiterate commission agent among sampled respondents is found in the Doaba zone, whereas the proportion of uneducated persons is 2.50 for the Majha and 2.22 for the Malwa zones of the state. The proportion of matriculate commission agents is high in the Doaba zone whereas the Majha and Malwa zones have the highest proportion of graduate commission agents.

Traditionally, two castes, namely the *Banias* and *Khatris* (*Aroras*), dominated in this business. However, presently, this business has not remained confined to these castes only. Although the dominant caste in this business is still the Bania, some new castes have entered in this business. Presently, 35 per cent commission agents belong to the Bania, about 27 per cent belong to the Jat, and 25 per cent belong to the Khatri caste. However, commission agents from some other castes like the *Brahmin, Rajput, Kamboj* and *Saini* are also involved in this business. This reveals that the capitalist development in agriculture has transformed the rigid caste-based arhtiya system to emerge as an economic or business profession.

The magnitude of commission agents in three agroclimatic zones clearly indicates that the commission agents from almost all the castes have been working in zone II. However in zone III, only Banias, Khatris and *Jats* are involved in this business. In zone I, the Jat is the dominant caste among commission agents (37.50%), followed by the Khatri (30%) and the Bania (10%). Similarly, the Jat caste is also dominant in zone II with 33.89 per cent, followed by the Bania with 27.78 per cent, the Khatri with 21.11 per cent, and the Brahmin with 12.22 per cent of commission agents. The scenario of zone III is entirely different, where the dominant caste of commission agents is Bania, not Jat. The cultural zone-wise scenario shows that Jat commission agents are dominant in Majha, Bania in the Malwa and Khatri in the Doaba zones of the state.

An average commission agent in Punjab State deals with

120 farmers of 71 families and serves farmers from 11 villages. About 44 per cent of the farmers are still dealing with the same commission agent for more than one generation. It is found that a commission agent in zone I deals with an average of 176 farmers from 112 farm families and serves around 26 villages. Similarly, in zone III, every commission agent deals with 130 farmers of 74 farm families from 6 villages. However, the number of farm families dealt with by a commission agent in zone II is 61 from 13 villages. This picture shows that the network of commission agents of zone I is widespread over a large number of farmers and in a large number of villages. The cultural zone-wise distribution shows that a commission agent of the Doaba zone deals on an average with 159 farmers of 94 farm families from 24 villages. Similarly, in the Malwa and Majha zones, every commission agent deals with 66 and 44 farm families from 8 and 9 villages, respectively. This shows that in the Doaba zone of Punjab, commission agents have a comparatively vast network in which a large number of farmers from many villages are covered.

The caste based occupation of moneylending is undergoing changes in recent years. Jat farmers have entered this occupation today and therefore it is no longer the monopoly of Banias. Despite the differences in farmers' perceptions of the caste background of the arhtiya, about 15 per cent of the farmers expressed their dislike of both the Bania and Jat caste arhtiyas; they preferred arhtiyas from other castes. More importantly, 18 per cent of the farmers don't prefer arhtiyas from any caste. This again indicates how important it is to dismantle the system.

The number of non-traditional commission agents has been increasing in the agricultural marketing of the state. The non-traditional commission agents who have joined this business after the initiation of the green revolution (mid-1960s) are 92.33 per cent. This is because of the fact that big farmers having large sized farms generated and invested surplus capital into more lucrative professions, namely the commission agent business. The highest proportion (73.91%) of traditional commission agents falls in zone II followed by zone I (17.39%) and zone III (8.70%). So far as the cultural zone-wise scenario is concerned, Malwa has the highest proportion of traditional commission agents (65.22%), followed by Doaba (30.43%) and Majha (4.35%). Out of the total non-traditional commission agents, about 46 per cent came from the farming population, about 24 per cent came from the grocering community, and the remaining from the service sector (accountants (*muneems*), traders, financers, and fertilizer/pesticide shop owners et cetera).

Before the green revolution, the Jat community was mainly engaged in the farming activities. It was observed in our field survey that 5 per cent of the respondent commission agents from Jat families entered into this profession during the 1970s. The process gained momentum after 1980 as 26.25 per cent and 52.50 per cent of the Jat families joined this business during the 1980s and 1990s, respectively. During this period, a huge agriculture surplus was generated with larger farmers but reinvestment opportunities within the sector were squeezing and the marginal profits from reinvestment in agriculture started declining. This is why the rich peasantry sought to invest in the non-farming sector. Although they invested in rice shellers, transport, farm input shops, commission agent businesses, et cetera, the commission agent business, being intimately related to agriculture, emerged as a prominent field.

The majority of the commission agents are not dependent on one business only; they have allied business activities. About 47 per cent of commission agents have one additional business, 10.33 per cent have two additional business activities, and 1.33 per cent of commission agents have three additional business activities along with the commission agent business. As an allied business, a majority of the commission agents are found doing farming (48%) followed by running grocery shops (22.29%), pesticide/fertilizer shops (17.71%), rice sheller (16.0%), and other activities like property dealing, transport, and brick kiln.

During the early phase of the green revolution, the commission was deducted from both the dealing parties (farmers and procurement agencies) by the commission agents. However, during the 1980s, the commission agents stopped deducting the commission from the large farmers. Deduction was sustained for the small farmers only. After the 1990s, the scenario has totally changed; commission agents have stopped charging commission from all categories of farmers. Now only procurement agencies pay commission to the commission agents. It is very interesting to know that the large farmers negotiate with the commission agents for getting some part of the commission from them.

A considerable change in the social behaviour of commission agents has also been noticed. Although the traditional commission agents were professionally cunning and tricky, they were sober and polite in their dealings. This picture has changed into rudeness and arrogance to some extent due to the entry of Jats into this profession. During the green revolution period, a majority of the commission agents participated in the socioreligious functions of the large farmers. This scenario has changed as the non-traditional commission agents, particularly Jats, invite all their client farmers, irrespective of their land holding size.

Some of the farmers (about 10%) sold their means of production including land, tractor, farm implements, and other assets like livestock, gold ornaments, and trees to repay the loan. A few of them sold their assets at distress prices due to the continuous pressure of the commission agents. It is mandatory for commission agents to issue J-Forms to the farmers (sellers) for the sale of farm produce. Yet some of the farmers are deprived of this right. The evasion of taxes and market fee is depriving the state of its revenue. Due to the non-availability of J-Forms, the farmers also bear losses as they are not able to take advantage of the 'bonus price' generally announced late or any other compensation given by the government. Multiple licensing is another prevalent malpractice through which commission agents exploit the state exchequer. An average commission agent family has 1.66 licenses in the state. This number is the highest in zone III (2.33), followed by zone II (1.46) and zone I (1.20).

An average commission agent has advanced loans of Rs. 65.74 lakh to farmers. The interest accrued on this amount becomes Rs. 15.78 lakh per annum. Some commission agents have disclosed that they also borrow money from large farmers, police officials, bureaucrats, and other servicemen.

The amount of commission which the commission agent deducts from the farmer in case of low market arrival, either due to low productivity or crop failure, is called damami. About 9 per cent farmers complained for this deduction.

Commission agents prefer to give articles rather than cash to the farmer. For this purpose, the 'slip mechanism' is being used for farmers to purchase necessary items from the agents' own shops or connected shops. Always, the price of these articles is higher than the prevailing market price and comparatively lower quality commodities are given to farmers through this slip mechanism. Almost all the farmers have mentioned this mechanism during the field survey.

There is a debate among academicians, farmers' organizations, and commission agents about the role of the commission agent system in the agricultural economy of the state. Although the commission agent business is considered an easy and lucrative venture by a majority (59%) of the commission agents in Punjab, 13 per cent of the respondents considered it a tough and risky job because they always put their money at risk. It is being presumed that the survival of the farmers is not possible without the commission agents.

However, the present study breaks this myth and shows that about 84 per cent of the farmers of Punjab State are not in favour of the present system of 'arhtiyas'; they are of the view that the commission agents system should be abolished by the government. The preferences of the farmers regarding the commission agent system show that nearly 90 per cent of large and semi-medium farmers prefer to abolish the commission agent system. About 31 per cent of the marginal farmers support the existing commission agent system. It is important to know that a vast majority of farmers, whether they are illiterate or educated, are not in favour of the present 'arhtiya system'. All the highly educated farmers expressed views against the commission system. It is also interesting to see that even illiterate persons (84.91%) were keen to abolish the 'arhtiya system'.

A large number of problems are being faced by the farmers in dealing with commission agents in the state. Recovery of loans before any payment is the main problem faced by 53.25 per cent of the respondent farmers. About 46 per cent of the farmers opined that the commission agents charge an exorbitant rate of interest on credit which varies from 24 per cent to 36 per cent. About 40 per cent of farmers complained that the commission agents supply poor quality farm inputs to the farmers. High prices of domestic articles, malpractices in weighing, and prices of the produce, delay in making the payment for their produce, the problem of damami, demanding signatures on blank promissory notes, and rude behaviour on the part the commission agents are the main problems highlighted by the respondent farmers.

The majority of commission agents are opposed to the direct payment system of crops, merely due to the fear of non-recovery of their loans. When the commission agents were asked about their reaction regarding the implementation of the direct payment system of crops in Punjab agriculture, a majority of the commission agents (57%)

opined that in such a situation they would leave this profession. However, about 37 per cent of commission agents said they would limit or stop the money advances to the farmers, and just 5.33 per cent of them have threatened to protest against this decision of the government.

About 93 per cent respondent farmers are of the view that the direct payment system will be beneficial for the peasantry of Punjab. It is observed that the direct payment system is highly supported by the large farmers (97.40%) followed by medium (96.67%), semi-medium (92.59%), small (91.57%), and marginal farmers (82.22%). This shows that as the farm size increases, the proportion of farmers preferring direct payment system also increases.

All the educated farmers support the direct payment of crops. It is interesting to note that the majority of the illiterate farmers (66.04%) are also in favour of direct payment for their produce through cheques. The direct payment system is mainly supported by the farmers below the age group of 50 years. Overall about 93 per cent of the farmers are in favour of the direct payment system. On the whole, it can be concluded that the perceptions of farmers regarding the direct payment system in agricultural marketing are significantly associated with the size of the land, education level, and age of the farmers.

In Punjab, about 77 per cent of the farmers have their own bank account. It is pertinent to note that 98 per cent of families of farmers in the state are dealing with the banks. This high proportion (98%) of the farming community that is already dealing with the banks refute the logic of arhtiyas for not making payments through cheques merely on the basis of fear/problems of farmers dealing with the banks.

The most important reason of the farmers for favouring the direct payment system in agricultural marketing is to get the full payment of the crops (83.5%), followed by redemption from the clutches of the commission agents

(82.0%), withdrawal of money as per their requirement (72.5%), and more transparency in accounts (70.5%). Similarly, another reason in support of the direct payment system is the availability of better quality inputs (69.5%) from independent sources. About 61 per cent of farmers held that they can repay the loan as per their repaying capacity. Even after having many points in favour of direct payment, it has been opposed by about 7 per cent of the farmers. About 6 per cent of the farmers opined that they would not be able to get money at any point of time whereas in the prevailing commission agent system they could get it at any time on easy terms. All these reasons mentioned by the farmers against the direct payment system raise a question mark on the efficiency of the banking system of the state. Basically, these views are given by the farmers in the context of prevailing conditions and functioning of the banking system. An efficient and farmer-friendly banking system may not only be the substitute for the commission agent system but also be an effective agent for solving all their problems related to the financial market.

## RECOMMENDATIONS

1. The study has highlighted that the commission agent system for agriculture in its present module is an exploitative mechanism. Some legal framework has been enacted and modified from time to time; even then, the modus operandi of commission agent finds many ways of exploitation. This continues even when the market is more or less a monopsonistic one as public agencies are the major buyers. Therefore, alternative marketing systems like the Direct State Procurement System and the Cooperative Marketing System should be developed. These systems will be beneficial for the producer, consumer, and the state. The commission charges will be saved, which can be

redistributed amongst the farmers, the consumer, and the state. The government can release its enhanced revenue for agricultural research institutes of the state for developing latest agricultural research technologies, which would be in the long-term interest of the farm economy.

2. The banking system should be made farmer-friendly. The institutional loans should be made available not only for productive purposes but for purposes of consumption also which include health, education, social festivities, and day-to-day needs. The assessment of loans should be made on the basis of the market price of their land and not on the basis of an arbitrary fixed value of the land. In this way, the farmers may get more amount of loan for the fulfillment of their needs. The cumbersome and costly credit delivery system should be improved so that the farmers can get adequate and timely loans with low transaction costs. The easy repayment facilities, along with rebates on interest rates for timely payment, should be encouraged so that the farmer can get the required amount of money from institutional sources rather than going to private moneylenders, who charge an exorbitant rate of interest along with committing other malpractices. Moreover, the institutional credit facilities should be extended to the rural areas. There should be a bank branch in every village. For withdrawal of money at every time, Automated Teller Machine (ATM) facilities should be provided in the village itself so that the farmers and other rural people may get money as and when require.

3. As far as the alterative marketing systems are developed, some immediate measures should be taken:
   *a)* The existing payment system, in which the payment of the farmers' produce is made through the commission agents, should be scrapped. There should be a direct payment to the farmers for the procurement of their produce. The procurement agencies should make the payment directly to the farmers through cheques. It is the fundamental right of every person to get the payment himself for the sale of his commodity. The market principle states that the buyer always makes the payment directly to the seller. This principle should hold good in the case of the farmers (sellers) and the purchasing agencies (buyers) in Punjab agriculture. The direct payment to farmers through cheques will create transparency in the accounts which would be beneficial to the society.
   *b)* The government machinery should be re-enforced to curb the malpractices of commission agents like not issuing J-Forms, multiple licensing, damami, dual arhat, et cetera. In the given socioeconomic and political structure of Punjab's economy, these policy recommendations will solve the problems of farmers with respect to the product and credit markets. In a nutshell, the alternative marketing systems will reduce the market imperfections, which will help improve economic conditions of the debt-ridden Punjab peasantry.

# References


Association for Democratic Rights (AFDR) (2000) *Suicides in rural areas of Punjab: A Report* (in Punjabi). Patiala: AFDR, District Unit, October.

Bhalla, G.S., S.L. Sharma, N.N. Wig, S. Mehta and P. Kumar, (1998) *Suicides in Rural Punjab*. Chandigarh: Institute for Development & Communication (IDC).

Deb, Sharmistha and Meenakshi Rajeev (2007) 'Banking on Baniyas for Credit', *Economic and Political Weekly*, Vol. XLII No. 4, pp. 280–3.

Calvert, H. (1922) 'Wealth and Welfare of Punjab', *Civil and Military Gazette*, Lahore.

Chahal, T.S. (2005) *Forced Fall: A Case of Punjab Farmers*. Amritsar: Institute of Development and Planning. .

Darling, M.L. (1925) *The Punjab Peasant in Prosperity and Debt*. Delhi: Oxford University Press.

Gill, Sucha Singh (2009) 'Do Away with Middlemen: Farmers Will Get More for Their Produce', *The Tribune*, Chandigarh, 8 July.

GoP (1998) 'Possibility to Reduce the Number of Intermediaries in Agricultural Marketing System in the State of Punjab', *Expert Committee Final Report Submitted to Government of Punjab (GoP)*, Chandigarh, 17 August.

GoI (2007–8) *Economic Survey*, Government of India (GOI), New Delhi.

GoP (2008) *Statistical Abstract of Punjab*, Government of Punjab (GoP), Chandigarh.

Iyer, G.K. and M.S. Manick (2000) *Indebtedness, Impoverishment and Suicides in Rural Punjab*. New Delhi: India Publishers and Distributors.

Johl, S.S. (2009) 'Direct Payments to Farmers: Government Must

Not Give in to Arhtiyas' Pressure', *The Tribune*, Chandigarh, 15 September.

Nath, Diwarka (1941) 'Moneylending Legislation and Rural Credit in the Punjab', *The Indian Society of Agricultural Economics*, Lahore, April, pp. 52–61.

NSSO (2005) 'Indebtedness of Farmer Households: Situation Assessment Survey of Farmers', 59th Round, June–Dec. 2003, National Sample Survey Organization (NSSO), Government of India, May.

P A U (2009) *Farmers' and Agricultural Labourers' Suicides Due to Indebtedness in the Punjab State: Pilot Survey in Bathinda and Sangrur Districts*. Ludhiana: Department of Economics and Sociology, Punjab Agricultural University (PAU). Submitted to the Government of Punjab in April.

Pomeranz, Kenneth (2007) 'A History of Capitalism', *Economic and Political Weekly*, Vol.XLII No. 9 pp. 752–4.

Rangi, P.S. and M.S. Sidhu (2005). *Role of Commission Agents in Agricultural Marketing in Punjab*. Research Report, Department of Economics and Sociology, Punjab Agricultural University, Ludhiana.

Reddy, S.T. Somashekhara (2007) 'Diary of a Moneylender', *Economic and Political Weekly*, Vol. XLII, No. 29, pp. 3037–43.

RBI (1991–2) *All India Debt and Investment Survey, Incidence of Indebtedness of Households*. RBI Bulletin, Government of India, Vol. 53 (5), May and Vol. 54, No. 2, February.

Satish, P. (2007) 'Agricultural Credit in the Post-Reform Era: A Target of Systematic Policy Coarctation', *Economic and Political Weekly*, Vol.XLII No. 26, pp. 2567–75.

Shah, Mihir, Rangu Rao and P.S. Vijay Shankar (2007): 'Rural credit in 20th Century India: Overview of History and Perspective', *Economic and Political Weekly*, Vol.XLII, No. 15, pp. 1351–64.

Shergill, H.S. (1998) *Rural Credit and Indebtedness in Punjab*. Chandigarh: Institute for Development & Communication.

Shergill, H.S. (2010) *Growth of Farm Debt in Punjab* 1997 to 2008. Chandigarh: Institute for Development & Communication.

Sidhu, R.S., Sukhpal Singh, A. Kaur and M. Goyal (2000) *Loans Overdue and Indebtedness in Punjab Agriculture—A Case of Cotton Belt*. Ludhiana: NABARD Chair Unit, Punjab Agricultural University. Singh Karam, Sukhpal Singh and H.S. Kingra (2007) *Status of Farmers Who Left Farming in*

*Punjab*. Research Report. The Punjab State Farmers' Commission, Government of Punjab.

Singh, Karam, Sukhpal Singh and H.S. Kingra (2009) 'Agrarian Crisis and Depeasantisation in Punjab: Status of Small/ Marginal Farmers Who Left Farming', *Indian Journal of Agricultural Economics*, Vol. 64, No 4, pp. 585–603.

Singh, Karam (2009) 'The Rural Urban Divide in Punjab: It is Widening Again', in *Globalization and Change*, Ghuman R.S., S. Singh and J.S. Brar (eds.) New Delhi: Rawat Publications.

Singh, Karam (2009) 'Agrarian Crisis in Punjab: High Indebtedness, Low Returns, and Farmers' Suicides', in *Agrarian Crisis in India*, D. Narasimha Reddy and Srijit Mishra (eds.), New Delhi: Oxford University Press, pp. 261–84.

Singh, Master Hari (1983) *Agrarian Scene in Rural Punjab Vol. I.* New Delhi: People's Publishing House.

Singh, Sukhpal (2010) *Land Market in Rural Punjab. Preliminary Survey*. Ludhiana: Department of Economic and Sociology, Punjab Agricultural University.

Singh, Sukhpal and M.S. Toor (2005) 'Agrarian Crisis with Special Reference to Indebtedness Among Punjab Farmers', *Indian Journal of Agricultural Economics*, Vol. 60, No. 3, pp. 335–46.

Singh, Sukhpal, M. Kaur and H.S. Kingra (2007) *Flow of Funds to Farmers and Indebtedness in Punjab*. Research Report, The Punjab State Farmers' Commission, Government of Punjab.

Singh, Sukhpal, M. Kaur and H.S. Kingra (2008) 'Indebtedness Among Farmers in Punjab', *Economic and Political Weekly*, Vol.XLIII, No. 26 & 27, 28 June, pp. 130–6.

Singh, Sukhpal, M. Kaur and H.S. Kingra (2009) 'Inadequacies of Institutional Agricultural Credit System in Punjab State', *Agricultural Economic Research Review*, Vol. 22, July–Dec. 309–18.

Thorburn, S.S. (1885) *Mussalmans and Moneylender in the Punjab*. William Blackwood & Sons, London

Willian Digby (1969): *Prosperous British India: A Revelation from Official Records*. New Delhi: Sagar Publications.

P S F C (2009) Initiatives: Addressing the Farmers' Problems. Report, Punjab State Farmers Commission (PSFC) Government of Punjab, September.

# Appendices

## APPENDIX I

## J-FORM

[See Rule 24 (14)]

**Sale Voucher for the seller**

Counterfoil

Book No. ____________________ Serial No. ____________________

Name of Market ______________ Date of Auction ____________

Name of Katcha Arhtiya ____________ Address of seller ______

Name of Seller ____________________________________________

| *Name of Commodity* | *Name of the buyer* | *Weight* | *Rate (Rs.)* | *Total (Rs.)* | *Incidental Charges* | *Net amount paid (Rs.)* |
|---|---|---|---|---|---|---|
| | | | | | | |

Signature of seller,
his agent or representative

Signature of Katcha Arhtiya

Note :-Where the agriculture produce, being vegetable or fruit is delivered, it shall not be necessary to fill the column 2 relating to name of buyer.

## APPENDIX II

## I-FORM

[See Rule 24 (12) and 24 (13)]

**Bill of Katcha Arhtiya**

Counterfoil

Book No. ____________

Serial No. ____________

Name of Market ____________

Name of Katcha Arhtiya ____________

Name of Buyer ____________ Dated ____________

| *Name of Commodity* | *Weight* | *Rate (Rs.)* | *Total Amount (Rs.)* | *Market Charges (Rs.)* | *Grand Total (Rs.)* |
|---|---|---|---|---|---|
| | | | | Commission____<br>Brokerage______<br>Palledari______<br>Filling & Sewing Charges<br>Other Charges___<br>Total__________ | |

Acknowledgement by the buyer

Signature of Katcha Arhtiya

## APPENDIX III

### Total Number of Pucca Arhtiya Licensees Different Markets in Punjab, 2008

| *District* | *Grain Market* | *Fruit & Vegetabel Market* | *Total* |
|---|---|---|---|
| **Zone- I** | | | |
| Rupnagar | 1 | 8 | 9 |
| Hoshiarpur | 73 | - | 73 |
| S. Bhagat S. Nagar | 75 | 47 | 122 |
| **Subtotal** | **149** | **55** | **204** |
| **Zone- II** | | | |
| Ludhiana | 176 | 9 | 185 |
| Moga | 117 | - | 117 |
| Barnala | 135 | 57 | 192 |
| Fatehgarh Sahib | 20 | 4 | 24 |
| Jalandhar | 104 | 315 | 419 |
| Kapurthala | 96 | 16 | 112 |
| Amritsar | 250 | 16 | 266 |
| Gurdaspur | 367 | 2 | 369 |
| Sangrur | 484 | 52 | 536 |
| Mohali | 29 | 9 | 38 |
| Tarn Taran | 497 | - | 497 |
| Patiala | 25 | 2 | 27 |
| **Subtotal** | **2300** | **482** | **2782** |

| *District* | *Grain Market* | *Fruit & Vegetabel Market* | *Total* |
|---|---|---|---|
| **Zone-III** | | | |
| Faridkot | 131 | - | 131 |
| Mukatsar | 106 | 88 | 194 |
| Bathinda | 281 | 183 | 464 |
| Mansa | 213 | 62 | 275 |
| Firozpur | 333 | 152 | 485 |
| **Subtotal** | **1064** | **485** | **1549** |
| **Total** | **3513** | **1022** | **4535** |

*Figures in the parenthesis are percentages*

*Source: Punjab Mandi Board, Chandigarh*